ELIZABETH G. HAINSTOCK has been actively involved with the Montessori method since 1960. She received her Montessori certification from the St. Nicholas Training Centre, London, and began giving classes for parents and teachers on the adaptation of the method to successful home use. She has taught in Montessori schools and used the method in Head Start and public school programs. In 1971 she served as Montessori consultant for the Department of Health, Education and Welfare in the formation of its Home Start program, and in 1973 was the recipient of the "Montessorian of the Year" award from the Universal Montessori Teachers Association. Ms. Hainstock has been a curriculum evaluator and volunteer teacher in California schools. She has been a contributing author to *Children's House* and *Woman's Day* magazines and has traveled extensively in the United States and abroad, lecturing, conducting study groups, and helping to start Montessori schools.

ALSO BY ELIZABETH G. HAINSTOCK

Teaching Montessori in the Home:
The Pre-School Years
(available in a Plume edition)

The Essential Montessori
(available in a Mentor edition)

TEACHING
Montessori
IN THE HOME

TEACHING
Montessori
IN THE HOME

The School Years

ELIZABETH G. HAINSTOCK

A PLUME BOOK

PLUME
Published by the Penguin Group
Penguin Books USA Inc., 375 Hudson Street, New York, New York 10014, U.S.A.
Penguin Books Ltd, 27 Wrights Lane, London W8 5TZ, England
Penguin Books Australia Ltd, Ringwood, Victoria, Australia
Penguin Books Canada Ltd, 10 Alcorn Avenue, Toronto, Ontario, Canada, M4V 3B2
Penguin Books (N.Z.) Ltd, 182–190 Wairau Road, Auckland 10, New Zealand

Penguin Books Ltd, Registered Offices: Harmondsworth, Middlesex, England

Published by Plume, an imprint of New American Library, a division of Penguin
Books USA Inc. Published by arrangement with the author.

First Plume Printing, March, 1978
11 13 15 17 19 18 16 14 12 10

REGISTERED TRADEMARK—MARCA REGISTRADA

Library of Congress Catalog Card Number: 72-117665

Printed in the United States of America
Illustrations by Lee Ames & Mel Erikson

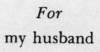

For
my husband

CONTENTS

In the words of the child:
"I hear and I forget.
I see and I remember.
I do and I understand."

TEACHING
Montessori
IN THE HOME

MONTESSORI IN THE HOME

This book, written as a sequel to *Teaching Montessori in the Home*, deals with mathematics and language development. In these major areas of education, it is vital that a solid background be attained for successful future learning. *Teaching Montessori in the Home* was an introduction to the Montessori method and the basic principles as applied for home use for children from the age of two through five. Much emphasis was placed on the preliminary preparation of the child through practical-life and sensorial exercises, which are a necessary prelude to further Montessori learning. Whereas my earlier book limited itself to working with the child at home in lieu of the school environment, this book is meant both to implement and supplement the schoolchild's education.

It is imperative in the overcrowded schools of today that no child be lost in the shuffle—especially yours. Furthermore, many school districts are constantly employing new and experimental methods of education. They may try one program one year, and another the next. As a result, many students have had no consistency in some areas of their education, and have been seriously hampered in their learning experiences. Sound progressive steps are indeed needed in education today, but experimentation must not take place at our children's expense. Statistics have made it all too clear that many children can muddle their way through several years, if not the whole duration, of schooling, without really understanding much of what it's all about. No longer is it good enough to simply enroll your child in P.S. 42 and then sit back awaiting optimal development of his potential. Parents must accept responsibility for their offspring's educational development. Most important, they must become aware of what is or is not being taught, even as early as the kindergarten level. It's too late to wait until your child experiences difficulties in high school subjects and then push the panic button as you discover that after many tedious years of schooling he's barely managed to acquire even the very basics of knowledge.

How much do you really know about what's going on in your child's classroom? Does he enjoy learning? If not, why not? Is he being allowed to utilize his potential to the best of his abilities? Or is he just drifting along the border of the nebulous abyss of nonlearning that soon will engulf too many of our children? What do those elementary-school report cards marked "Satisfactory" or "Needs improving" really tell us? Are your parent-teacher conferences full of smiles and clichés about what a sweet child you have, rather than remarks on his academic achievements? Pay attention before it's too late! Your children don't *have* to be on the losing end of the education spectrum. Very few children today glide through school with ease, and yet they can, with very little effort, look ahead to many years of happy learning if they are given a good foundation and the inner confidence that comes from fully understanding what's being taught. It's just human nature to enjoy what comes easily to us.

As Dr. Montessori believed, education begins at birth. Educating the human potential is a challenge that must be faced early if it is to be successful.

The ages given with each of the following exercises denote the ages that the specific lessons would be taught if the child were following a continuing Montessori education. In public schools today, however, learning is not quite this accelerated, and for this reason, the lessons are appropriate for children through junior high school if they have particular problems in math or English. Do not be misled by the ages given with the exercises in working with your own child. Remember that it is not your child's chronological age that should guide you, but rather the child himself—his abilities, background, readiness and difficulties. The important thing for *all* children, whether they are six or sixteen, is to know the fundamentals of mathematics and language so that they may better understand and succeed in the more advanced concepts. A good illustration of this is the experience of a group of remedial reading teachers with whom I recently worked. The bulk of their third-grade reading class, in an underprivileged area, could not read at even the first-grade level. Rather than simply brand these children as being slow or as having below-average intelligence, the teachers pursued the problem further and discovered that the children could not read because they had never been taught the fundamental alphabet sounds. Rather than continuing with a program meant for eight-year-olds, they began at the beginning. Using the Montessori sandpaper letters usually used with three- and four-year-olds, they gradually established a framework on which these children could build until their proper reading level was attained.

Just as there are no firm rules or ages for these exercises, there is no rigid schedule for teaching them. The child may work with them at will and as the necessity arises. Once a child enters school his free hours are limited and varied, so that time for extra activities must be flexible. I have often cooked breakfast while one of my children was dividing pegs between markers on the kitchen floor to really "see" a division problem.

Do not allow your child to feel pressured or overburdened in his work, or his enthusiasm for learning will stop and he will become resentful of the extra exercises and your help. You must be able to sense the child's attitude and proceed accordingly. Take your lead from the child and remember always that he is an individual with many needs and moods. The quality of the work taught and its relevance to the situation are what's important, and your own sensitivity and timing will be important to the child's real learning.

Exercises may be taught as an introduction to the corresponding type of work that will be learned at school, as background material to establish a solid understanding and working knowledge of a particular area, as reinforcement in weak areas, or simply as supplemental work for the overachieving but understimulated student. The materials must always be properly demonstrated, however, before the child is left to work on his own. It is vital that the child fully understand what he is doing before going on to a more advanced, but related, exercise. The sequential learning patterns inherent in Montessori's teaching must be adhered to, for good learning comes through repetition and repeated handling of the materials as the child sees and understands for himself the why and wherefore.

A parent may work with a child who has not yet entered first grade to continue work begun in *Teaching Montessori in the Home*. The older child in school may be helped in difficult areas by the parent, and in many cases the child of twelve or over can follow the text of this more advanced book himself.

To use the book successfully, whether at home or in a school situation, read it first for general knowledge and understanding. Then go through the contents and find the areas in which your child needs help. For example, if a ten-year-old is experiencing difficulty with multiplication, begin with the first exercise listed for multiplication and let the child set the pace. In a situation that requires using numbers in various ways, be sure that the child has a solid grasp of the most elementary workings of the numbers one through ten.

Remember to let the child always proceed at his own pace, learning and discovering as much as possible on his own. Be available when help is needed. But resist the temptation to interfere and constantly interject well-meant but disruptive advice and help. Minimize your child's errors and correct them without making him feel incapable or foolish. The patience, interest and enthusiasm you show toward his achievements will greatly influence his desire to learn. Your child should continue to think of learning as an exciting and challenging experience. If the materials described in this book are properly presented to him, he'll do just that. And he will acquire the solid bases for reading, writing and mathematics needed in the years ahead.

THE THREE-PERIOD LESSON

The purpose of the Three-Period Lesson is to teach new concepts in a repetitive way, thereby helping the child to better understand the materials as they are presented. This also aids the teacher in seeing how well the child is grasping and absorbing what is being shown to him. These three steps should be used with every initial demonstration of the mathematics and language lessons included in this book. Three or four objects are usually used at a time. If the child does not seem to understand one of the periods, begin again, always making sure that one step is fully understood before going on to the next.

First Period: Recognition of identity
Make the association between the object being shown and its name. "This is ———."
Second period: Recognition of contrasts
To make sure that the child understands, say, "Give me the ———."
Third period: Discrimination between similar objects
To see if the child remembers the name himself, point to the various objects, saying, "Which one is this?"

□

Mathematics

INTRODUCTION

The basis for a child's early learning in mathematics and numbers should be established by the time he is three years old. With the infant, such simple games as counting his toes or fingers is a good beginning. Take advantage of everything in the child's environment. Count the steps to the front door, the bottles of milk the milkman left, the trees on the block, the daisy plants Dad is putting in the garden. Opportunities for stimulating number awareness are endless. When numbers are discussed as part of the daily routine the child will soon begin counting things himself as he plays. Use things in which the child is interested as your key. My eldest daughter, an avid television fan, learned the channel numbers first, as they were of prime interest. Then she became fascinated with clocks and telling time. She often came to me and asked, "What time is it when the little hand is on Channel four and the big hand is on Channel two?" Numbers are around us everywhere: time, money, size, age, date, cookies, eggs. Only an extremely unaware child can reach his third birthday with lack of knowledge of at least a few numbers and what they represent.

At age three, the child's interest in numbers is keen. The time has come to begin making orderly and clear number concepts from these facts that he vaguely understands. At first the child is not intellectually aware of number concepts, but he is beginning to be aware of quantity. Now is the time to introduce formal number learning, which provides the basis for mathematics.

Through the earliest sensorial training (of the kind detailed in my earlier book, *Teaching Montessori in the Home*), the numeration process has gradually been built up in the child's mind. Through a steady progressive sequence, he has seen how the process works and taught himself through manipulative learning. Inherent in all of the sensorial apparatus was the idea of quantity and the conception of identity, similarity and difference. The child, for example, sees in the cubes of the tower the gradual built-up of size, laying the foundation for the same process to be repeated in actual numbers.

The decimal system is the basis for our numbers system. Therefore, a thorough knowledge of the numbers one through ten—the written number and the quantity represented by that number—is necessary if the child is to grasp fully any future mathematical problem. By using manipulative materials to learn the fundamental concepts of mathematics at an early age, the child assimilates easily the basic facts and skills. Children need to be able to move the items as they count them to gain a real understanding of the quantities. The satisfaction of discovery leads to an enthusiastic interest in numbers when the child is able to demonstrate the fundamental mathematical operation, rather than simply being told seemingly dull and meaningless facts. He physically holds the quantities that he sees represented by written symbols. He combines the materials, counts, separates and compares them while visually grasping and reinforcing the ideas in a way that is concrete, rather than abstract. The teacher gives the child a given concept and lets him reach the realization through working at his own speed. In this way the child sees and understands the relationships between numbers, and also absorbs the idea that the value of a number is indicated by the position in which it is written. First the quantity names are taught; then the quantity symbol; finally the two are combined.

By using the many different materials available for the various mathematical processes, the child is repeatedly given variations on one central theme: understanding the working function of the numbers one through ten. By handling the materials and using them in many different ways, concepts not obvious at first glance become apparent as the child not only sees the fundamental ideas but discovers new ones. Through repetition, facts are understood rather than simply memorized. And as the necessary operations are performed, a sound working knowledge is instilled of what each operation means.

Before beginning the mathematics exercises on the following pages, a thorough concept of the numbers one through ten must have been learned previously through work with the number rods, spindle box and sandpaper numbers described in my first book, *Teaching Montessori in the Home*.

The material to be used with this book is varied. The Golden Bead material, which is used for many different exercises in mathematics, was originated by Dr. Montessori, who chose gold for its mellow and pleasing color. It seems always to be a favorite among the children. The beads are easy to handle, and they present the various concepts so clearly that the child's interest in numbers is easily stimulated. The introduction to the Golden Bead material is the presentation of quantity names: unit, ten, hundred and thousand. The child sees the beads that represent these quantities and their relationships. Each is made up of ten of the previous quantity. The ten-bar is composed of ten units; the hundred-square is made up of 10 ten-bars; and the thousand-cube is equivalent to 10 hundred-squares. The terms *unit, ten, hundred* and *thousand* are used to give meaning to the beads as the child sees the build-up of higher quantities. The child sees and understands that there are never more than nine in a group. Simple numbers are used at first ("Bring me four units," "Bring me three tens," etc.), then numbers are combined ("Bring me four hundreds, three tens and eight units"). Eventually, large quantities are combined on the tray, separated and categorized.

Presentation of the written number symbol comes with the number-symbol cards. These cards are printed in different colors indicating the columns of the decimal system. The units are in green, the tens in blue, the hundreds in red. The thousands are in green again, because in the Montessori method they are considered the units of the next number sequence. The child sees the symbol for the bead quantities with which he has worked and associates the quantity and written symbol. As the larger number combinations are introduced, the child is shown how to superimpose the symbol cards. Rather than 4,000, 200, 80, 5, he sees that the number is written as 4285. The idea of place value is also reinforced, and the concept of numbers broadened.

Gradually the complicated ideas of "changing," "borrowing" and "taking away" are easily formulated in the child's mind as he handles the beads. Through addition and multiplication of the beads, the combining of quantities to form larger quantities becomes readily apparent. Conversely, the child sees that subtraction is the breaking up of a large number into smaller ones. Division implies sharing, so the answer is always shown by what one person has received.

Through the use of the ten-bars and unit-beads and the first set of Seguin boards,* the "teen" numbers are taught. The child sees that eleven is made up of ten plus one, twelve is ten plus two, and so on. The second set of Seguin boards introduces the numbers 21 to 99 in the same way. At this time, the child also learns the conventional terms of quantity: ten, twenty, thirty. (Up to this point, he has referred to them as one ten, two tens, three tens.) The names of the quantities and the sequence of numbers are seen and reinforced in the child's mind.

---

* These boards were devised by Édouard Seguin, a French psychiatrist who taught mental defectives.

To repeat, mathematical facts are never simply memorized; the child assimilates them by using the appropriate manipulative materials. These problems, once worked, can be written on paper. The snake game is a preparation for learning the addition tables. The short bead stair is also used for addition, and the various bead quantities are represented by colors.

The problems of addition, subtraction, multiplication and division understood earlier through use of the Golden Bead material are now reinforced by symbols with the charts and boards for the processes. These provide a systematic means of learning, understanding and later memorizing the tables.

The bead frames present the more abstract concepts of addition, subtraction and multiplication. The child develops the concept of computation, numeration and notation necessary for higher mathematics.

Through the use of the fraction materials, the child sees how a whole may be divided into parts. At first, this is more of a visual exercise than an intellectual one. But through handling of the fractional insets, the child becomes familiar with fractions and their composition. The written symbols for the fractions are introduced and simple problems are worked.

An introduction to factoring and finding multiples is also given to familiarize the child with terminology.

Use the Three-Period Lesson with all initial introductory work to be sure that the child understands what is being taught. Proceed at the child's own pace, and on his level of attainment, and his enthusiasm and progress will be gratifying to both of you.

MATERIALS:

HOW TO MAKE THEM

TRAYS:

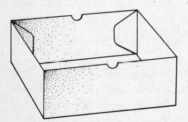

Wooden trays are usually used for the work with the Golden Bead material. Extra ones may be used to represent additional children in the exercises if you are working with just one child. The trays should be of a size easily handled by the child and yet with enough room for the bead material. A piece of felt or terry cloth should be placed on the bottom of the tray to keep the beads from sliding around. A sturdy gift-box lid, with low sides, or a baking pan make good tray substitutes.

MATS:

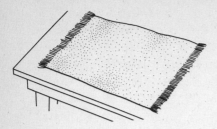

Cloth mats to put on the table-top to make working easier. A piece of felt the size of the small tabletop, or approximately 33" × 18", is adequate. A hand towel is also good. A large mat for the floor can also be made from felt.

THE GOLDEN BEAD MATERIAL:*

unit   ten bar

The golden beads are small beads, approximately ¼". They are usually made of ceramic, plastic or other synthetic material. The units are represented by individual beads. The tens are represented by a ten-bar (ten unit-beads strung on a small wire) and the hundreds are made up of 10 ten-bars wired together to form a square. The thousands are represented by a cube formed by wiring 10 hundred-squares together. You may string inexpensive dime-store beads or make representations of the beads by using graph paper and cardboard or balsa wood. For the unit-beads, cut 100 individual ¼" squares of graph paper. For the ten-bars, cut ten strips of ten squares each. For the hundred-squares, cut ten 10" × 10" squares. For the thousand-cubes, use 10" × 10" squares to paste on the sides of a cube made of cardboard or

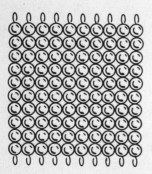

hundred square

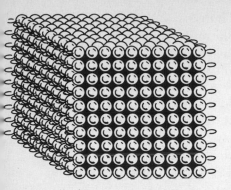

thousand cube

balsa wood. The units, bars, squares and cubes should be glued to cardboard for durability. This quantity is the minimum requirement of Golden Bead material needed in the exercises. More can be made for a wider range of use with such exercises as the Bank Game and for the addition, subtraction, multiplication and division exercises.

* The Golden Bead material is a necessary and integral part of Montessori mathematics.

THE SHORT BEAD STAIR:

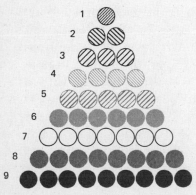

The short bead stair is a set of nine bead bars, each bar made up of colored beads as follows:

1 red, 2 green, 3 pink, 4 yellow, 5 light blue, 6 brown, 7 white, 8 violet, 9 dark blue.

These may be cut from 1/4" graph paper like the Golden Bead material, with each bead represented by a square and colored as noted above. There should be two sets of them.

THE BLACK AND WHITE BEAD BARS:

The black and white bead bars consist of a set of nine bead bars, made up of black and white beads as follows:
Bars 1-5—all black beads,
Bar 6—five black beads and one white bead,
Bar 7—five black beads and two white beads,
Bar 8—five black beads and three white beads,
Bar 9—five black beads and four white beads.

THE NUMBER-SYMBOL CARDS:

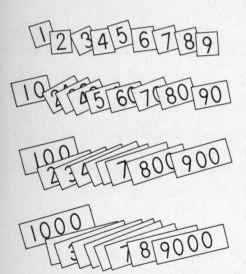

These cards represent the written number symbols. There are at least two sets of large cards and three sets of small cards. The large cards should all be 2½″ × 2″ high. Using heavy white construction paper, cut nine unit cards, 2½″ × 2″ and write the numbers 1 to 9 with a green felt pen. Cut nine 2½″ × 4″ cards and use a blue pen to write the tens from 10 to 90. Cut nine 2½″ × 6″ cards and with a red pen write the hundreds from 100 to 900. Cut nine 2½″ × 8″ cards and with a green pen write the thousands from 1000 to 9000. Line up the numerals evenly. The small cards are made the same way, but the sizes should be 1¼″ × 1″, 1¼″ × 2″, 1¼″ × 3″, and 1¼″ × 4″.

THE SEGUIN BOARDS:

These number boards are made of wood and are used for teaching the numbers from 10 to 99. They are long, narrow boards divided into equal sections by narrow wooden horizontal strips of grooved wooden molding.

The Teen Board:

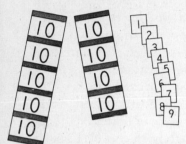

To teach the teen numbers from 10 to 19, two boards are used. The first board has five equal parts, the second four. Each section has a large 10 written on it. There are nine number cards, 1 to 9. Each card should be approximately 3″ × 2″ so that it can be slipped over the 0 of the 10.

The Ten Board:

To teach the numbers 10 to 90, two boards are used. The first board has five equal parts numbered 10 to 50; the second has four equal parts numbered 60 to 90. The nine number cards, 1 to 9, used with the teen board, can also be used with these boards. The boards can be made of masonite with grooved-wood molding dividers for the number cards to be slid in and out. The boards can also be cut from poster board and divided by lines, and the number cards set in place.

ADDITION STRIP BOARD:

This board is divided into squares, eighteen across and ten down. The numbers 1 to 10 are printed across the top in red, the numbers 11 to 18 are also written across the top, but in blue. A red vertical line divides the board after the ten. There are two sets of strips, one red and one blue. Each set has nine strips, increasing in length from the size of one square to the size of nine squares. The numbers 1 to 9 are written on the end of each appropriate strip.

The strip board is best made from a piece of poster board approximately 16″ × 10″, divided into ¾″ squares. The strips may be cut from poster board or light cardboard.

1	2	3	4	5	6	7	8	9	10	11	12	13	14	15	16	17	18

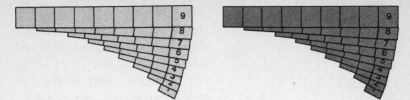

ADDITION CHARTS:

There are two addition charts, each divided vertically and horizontally into ten equal squares. The numbers 0 to 9 are written in black ink across the top and also down the left-hand side. One chart is filled in (it is shown in the Appendix); the other is left blank.

The charts can be made from cardboard or construction paper, approximately 8″ square and divided into ¾″ squares.

0	1	2	3	4	5	6	7	8	9
1									
2									
3									
4									
5									
6									
7									
8									
9									

SUBTRACTION STRIP BOARD:

This board is approximately 15″ × 3″. Across the center are eighteen ¾″ squares numbered 1 to 9 in blue and 10 to 18 in red. A blue vertical line is drawn after the nine-square. There is one set of nine blue rulers, increasing in length from the size of one square to the size of nine squares, made the same way as the addition board. There is one white ruler which is the length of seventeen squares.

The subtraction strip board can be made with the same materials as the addition strip board.

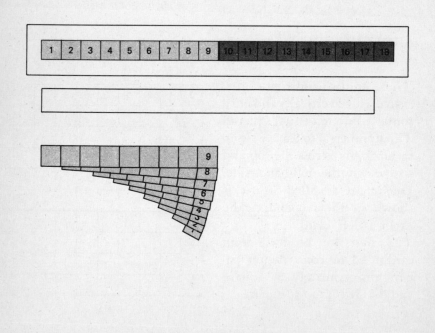

SUBTRACTION CHARTS:

There are two subtraction charts, each divided into ¾" squares numbered 9 to 18 across the top, 9 to 1 from top to bottom down the left side and −9 through −1 from top to bottom down the right-hand side. One chart has the answers filled in, as shown in the Appendix, and is referred to as the subtraction summary chart. The other is blank. Shirt cardboard is a good size for charts, or heavier poster board can be used.

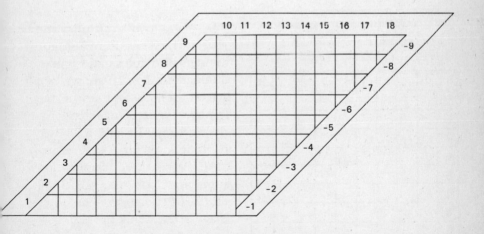

COMBINATION AND ANSWER SLIPS:

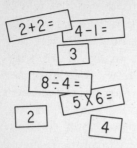

The combination slips are made from pieces of paper, approximately 2″ × ¾″, on which are written all the individual addition, subtraction, multiplication and division combinations from 1 through 9. The answers to these problems are written on pieces of paper half the length of the combination slips.

SUM BOOKS:

The sum books are small booklets of ten single pages, approximately 2″ × 3″, on which addition and subtraction problems without answers are written. The combinations can be of your choice.

MULTIPLICATION CHARTS:

1	2	3	4	5	6	7	8	9	10
2									
3									
4									
5									
6									
7									
8									
9									
10									

There are two multiplication charts which consist of a square divided into 100 small squares. The figures 1 to 10 are written across the top and down the left-hand side. One chart has the answers filled in, as shown in the Appendix, and is referred to as the multiplication summary chart, also called the table of Pythagoras. The other chart is left blank.

Poster board or construction paper approximately 8″ to 10″ square, divided into smaller ¾″ squares, is sufficient.

**MULTIPLICATION
BOARD:**

This board is a wooden or cardboard square with ten rows of ten holes. The numbers 1 to 10 are written across the top. Midway down the left-hand side is a square into which the small number cards can be slipped.

A piece of pegboard from a hardware store is ideal for making the board. Small 1"-square number cards from 1 to 10 can be cut from paper and placed on the designated area to the left of the board. One hundred pegs or beads are used, and a disk or button is used as a counter. A square of poster board or paper can also be used, with dots representing the holes, and beans used in place of the pegs.

MULTIPLICATION SUM CARDS:

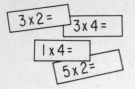

These sum cards are made from sheets of paper with the various multiplication tables written on them, without answers. Individual slips of paper with the combinations can also be used.

SHORT-DIVISION BOARD:

The short-division board is a wooden, cardboard square or pegboard with nine rows of nine holes. There are nine larger holes at the top of the board numbered 1 to 9. The numbers 1 to 9 are also written down the left-hand side of the board.

Items required are three boxes of red, blue and green pegs, and skittles or some other type of marker, such as beans or buttons.

DIVISION CHARTS:

The two division charts should be made from cardboard or construction paper, approximately 24″ × 8″, with ½″ squares. The numbers, perfectly divisible, and their divisors, from 1 ÷ 1 to 81 ÷ 9, are written as pictured. One chart is blank; the other, which has the answers filled in, is referred to as the division summary chart, and is shown in the Appendix.

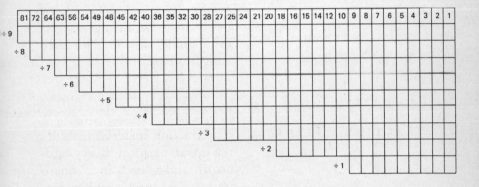

DIVISION SUM CARDS:

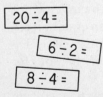

The division sum cards are made from small slips of paper on which are written the individual combinations of perfectly divisible problems (e.g., 20 ÷ 4, 6 ÷ 2, etc.).

BEAD FRAME:

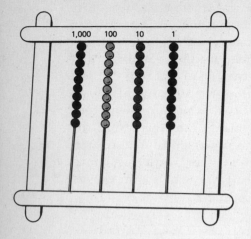

The short bead frame is a 10"-square frame of wood, with four vertical wires at equal intervals. The first wire to the right contains ten green beads, representing units. The next wire has ten blue beads, representing tens. The third wire has ten red beads, representing hundreds. The wire on the far left has ten green beads, repsenting thousands.

This frame may be made from ¾" strips of wood forming a square. Inexpensive ½" plastic beads may be strung on medium-grade wire or wire coathanger strips.

FRACTION MATERIAL:

The fraction material includes ten metal, plastic or heavy cardboard circles, each in a square frame. The circles and frames are of contrasting colors. The first circle is a whole, the second is divided into halves, etc., up through the tenth circle, which is divided into ten equal pieces. Each fraction of the circle has a small knob or handle for grasping.

These circles may be cut from

poster board, using a 5″ square for the frame and circles with a 3½″ diameter. Small beads or pieces of towel may be glued to the pieces for knobs.

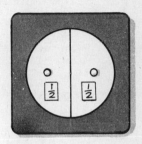

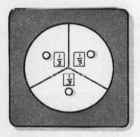

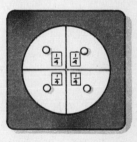

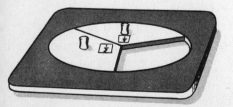

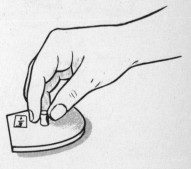

FRACTION CARDS:

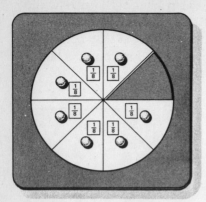

There are two sets of fraction cards. They are small cards, approximately ¼" square, cut to fit on the fractional parts of the circles described above. One set is marked to match the individual fractional parts (e.g., ½, ⅓, etc.). The other set, approximately ½" square, is marked to represent the combinations of fractional parts (e.g., ⅔, ¾, etc.).

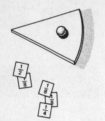

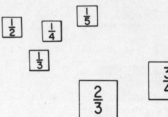

FRACTION BOOKLETS:

These fraction booklets are small booklets approximately 3" × 2", each with six to eight pages. On one side of each page is written a fraction problem to be solved. There are several of these fraction booklets for addition, subtraction, multiplication and division, going from easy to difficult problems. There are also several books containing fractions to be reduced to their lowest common denominators.

**FACTOR AND
MULTIPLES BOARD:**

This is a square board, perforated with 900 small holes, 30 rows of 30. A pegboard may be used with differently colored pegs. A large square of construction paper with the holes represented by dots can be substituted, with beans or similar objects used in place of pegs.

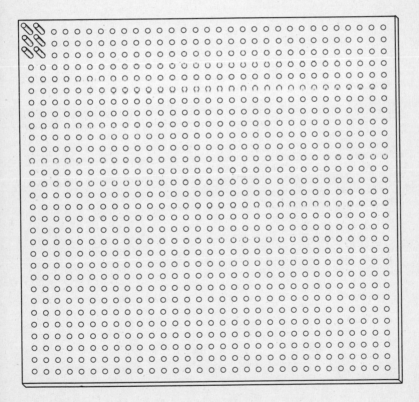

EXERCISES

THE GOLDEN BEAD MATERIAL
Age 4½–6

MATERIAL
EXERCISE I:

Small cloth mat for table.
1 unit-bead.
1 ten-bar.
1 hundred-square.
1 thousand-cube.

DEMONSTRATION:

1) Place the mat on the table and the materials to one side of it.

2) Place the unit-bead in front of the child and say, "This is one unit."

3) Place the ten-bar in front of the child and say, "This is ten."

4) Place the hundred-square in front of the child and say, "This is one hundred."

5) Place the thousand-cube in front of the child and say, "This is one thousand."

6) Place all the bead material in front of the child and point out (or let him discover) that the ten-

bar is composed of 10 unit-beads, the hundred-square is composed of 10 ten-bars and the thousand-cube is composed of 10 hundred-squares.

7) Use the Three-Period Lesson.

PURPOSE:

To learn the names *unit, tens, hundreds, thousands.*

To show that each is made up of ten of the preceding denomination.

MATERIAL EXERCISE II:

Small cloth mat for table.

9 unit-beads.

9 ten-bars.

9 hundred-squares.

1 thousand-cube.

DEMONSTRATION:

1) Place the mat on the table and the necessary materials to the side of it.

2) Begin with the unit-beads, laying them out one at a time, as if you were making a ten-bar, counting them out loud as you do so, e.g., "One, two . . ."

3) Lay out the last unit-bead and say, "Nine." Picking up a ten-bar, say, "There are no more single units, so I will use ten."

4) Place the ten-bar to the left of the units, saying, "One ten."

5) Continue placing the ten-bars, as if making a hundred-square, saying aloud, "Two tens, three tens," etc. When you reach "nine tens,"

say, "If I had one more, it would be ten tens or one hundred."

6) Place 1 hundred-square to the left of the tens. Pile the hundred-squares one on top of the other, counting aloud, "Two hundreds, three hundreds . . ."

7) "Nine hundreds. If I had one more, it would be ten hundreds, or one thousand." Place the thousand-cube to the left of the hundreds.

8) Now invite the child to do it by himself.

PURPOSE: To reinforce the relationship between units, tens, hundreds, thousands.

MATERIAL
EXERCISE III: Large mat for the floor.
9 unit-beads.
9 ten-bars.
9 hundred-squares.
9 thousand-cubes.
A tray.

DEMONSTRATION: 1) Place the mat on the floor and the unit-beads out from top to bottom about two inches apart, counting aloud.

2) Lay the ten-bars side by side, next to the units.

3) Next to the ten-bars, lay the hundred-squares, then the thousand-cubes.

4) Give the child a tray and ask him

to bring you a certain number of beads. As the beads are brought to you, check the number, then have the child return them and bring another number.

5) Begin simply; for example: "Please bring me two hundreds." Later ask him to bring larger combinations: "Bring me two thousands, four hundreds, three tens and four units."

6) When the child seems proficient at this, let two children play together, one asking for the beads, the other getting them.

PURPOSE:

To help the child understand the decimal system.

To give the child practice in working with the numbers and understanding directions.

NUMBER-SYMBOL CARDS

Age 4½–6

MATERIAL EXERCISE I: The large number-symbol cards for numbers 1, 10, 100, 1000.

DEMONSTRATION:
1) Place the 1 card in front of the child, saying, "This is how we write one unit."
2) Place the 10 card in front of the child saying, "This is how we write ten."
3) Continue in this way with the "hundred" card and the "thousand" card.
4) Use the Three-Period Lesson.

PURPOSE: To show how the quantities are written.

MATERIAL EXERCISE II: The large symbol cards 1 to 9, 10 to 90, 100 to 900, 1000 to 9000.

DEMONSTRATION: Proceed in the same manner with the cards as you did with the beads in Exercise II of the Golden Bead material.

PURPOSE: To show how the quantities are written.
To reinforce the relationship between units, tens, hundreds, thousands.

MATERIAL EXERCISE III:	The large symbol cards 1 to 9, 10 to 90, 100 to 900, 1000 to 9000.
DEMONSTRATION:	Proceed in the same manner with the cards as you did with the beads in Exercise III (steps 4 to 6) of the Golden Bead material.
PURPOSE:	To give the child more familiarity with how the quantities are written.

MATERIAL EXERCISE IV:

The Golden Bead material:
9 unit-beads
9 ten-bars
9 hundred-squares
9 thousand-cubes
A tray.
All the number-symbol cards: 1 to 9, 10 to 90, 100 to 900, 1000 to 9000.

DEMONSTRATION:

1) Set the numbers and the beads up as in Step II. Place all the Golden Bead material and number-symbol cards on the table.

2) Give the child a tray with a number-symbol card on it and ask him to bring you that quantity of beads, beginning with simple combinations (e.g., 200) and working up to the more complex (e.g., 3248).

3) As the beads are brought to you, count and arrange them neatly. As you say the number, superimpose the symbol cards (e.g., 2000, 300, 20, 6 become 2326).

4) Reverse the procedure, giving the child a certain number of beads and asking him to bring you the number-symbol card for them.

5) This may be done with a group of children.

PURPOSE:

To understand the relationship between the quantities and written numbers.

MATERIAL
EXERCISE V:

The Golden Bead Material:
45 unit-beads
45 ten-bars
45 hundred-squares
45 thousand-cubes

All the number-symbol cards 1 to 9, 10 to 90, 100 to 900, 1000 to 9000. This exercise is optional; it can be used to reinforce relationships between quantities and written numbers, if the necessary amount of materials or substitutes are available.

DEMONSTRATION:

1) Have the child place all the unit-symbol cards on the floor, one by one, while saying the number aloud.

2) Tell him to lay next to them the corresponding number of unit-beads.

3) Have him proceed in this manner for all the cards and Golden Bead material until they are all laid out.

PURPOSE: To associate the numbers with the quantities.

To reinforce the idea of the place value of the decimal system.

Familiarity with the Golden Bead material for later use with mathematics operations.

THE BANK GAME

Age 4½–6

MATERIAL: All the Golden Bead material.

All the large number cards up to 9000.

DEMONSTRATION:
1) Lay the cards out on a table, and the bead material on another table called the Bank.
2) Place a jumbled quantity of beads on the tray and take it to the child's table.
3) Remove the beads from the tray one by one, sorting them so that all the units are together, as are the ten-bars, hundred-squares and thousand-cubes.

4) Count the beads, beginning with the units. Each time there are more than nine in any group go to the bank and exchange them for one of the next (e.g., 34 units become 3 tens and 4 units, 12 tens become 1 hundred and 2 tens, etc.).

5) Place the appropriate number cards by the beads, say the quantities aloud, then superimpose the number cards (e.g., 3000, 700, 80, 5 become 3785).

6) Once the child understands the process, he may work with one or more other children, if there is a classroom situation. One child could be "banker," another handle the numbers and another do the bead work. Often a child will want to make an elaborate-looking number and then find that number of beads. This is all right too.

PURPOSE:

Further practice with the decimal system.
Understanding that there are never more than nine in a group.
Preparation for addition.

ADDITION

Age 5–7

MATERIAL:
Three sets of the small number-symbol cards.
One set of the large number-symbol cards.
Three trays.
All Golden Bead material.

DEMONSTRATION:

1) Place the small and large number-symbol cards on a table.

2) Have the bead material on another table.

3) Place a number (superimposed with the small number-symbol cards) on the first child's tray and ask him to go to the Bank and take that number of beads.

4) Send a second child to the Bank for another number of beads, indicated by another superimposed card.

5) As the children return with their beads, check the number, and place the first group of beads and number on the table, with the second group under them—all the units on the right, tens to the left, etc.

6) Count the beads, beginning with the units, and exchange where necessary.

7) When the units are counted, take that number from the large number-symbol cards and place it on the table; continue this with the other cards. Superimpose the cards for your total.

8) Begin with two simple addends (using numbers with no carrying, e.g., 1231 + 342). Then use numbers where carrying is necessary (e.g., 4295 + 1687). Then use three or four addends.

9) After this initial introduction and some supervision, several children may work together.

PURPOSE: Understanding how the decimal system is used in addition.

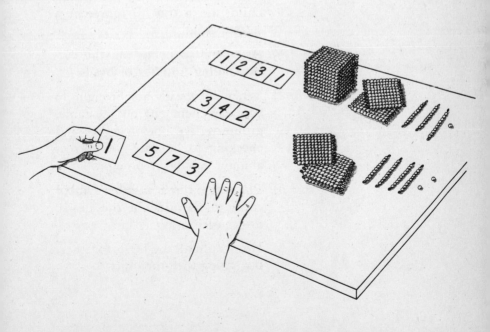

MULTIPLICATION

Age 5½–7

MATERIAL:
All Golden Bead material.
1 set of large number-symbol cards.
Three sets of small number-symbol cards.
Trays.

DEMONSTRATION:

1) Place all cards on one table and beads on another.

2) From the set of small number-symbol cards, give each child (two children at first) the same number, e.g., 324. If there is only one child, use a tray to represent a second child.

3) Ask them to bring you the corresponding number of beads.

4) When the beads are brought to you, lay them out on the table, grouping like ones together and checking to be sure the correct amount has been brought.

5) Place the small number-symbol cards to the side of the beads, under each other.

6) Now count all the beads together, beginning with the units.

7) As each group is counted, get the proper number-symbol card from the large cards. Count the units and get the 8 card, count the tens and get the 40 card, count the hundreds and get the 600 card. Now the child can see that $324 \times 2 = 648$.

8) When the children have done several simple problems, begin using numbers that involve changing. Then have more children join the group and multiply by larger numbers, always using the same number of children that the number is to be multiplied by. Again, if only one child is being taught, use trays to represent the multiplier.

PURPOSE:

To show that multiplication forms a larger quantity by bringing together the same quantity several times.
To illustrate the process of multiplication by using the decimal system.

SUBTRACTION
Age 5½–7

MATERIAL:

All Golden Bead material.
One set of large number-symbol cards.
Two sets of small number-symbol cards.
Two trays.

DEMONSTRATION:

1) Place the small and large number-symbol cards on a table.

2) Place a number of beads on the table, with the corresponding number in large number-symbol cards to the side.

3) Use the small number-symbol cards to place a number on the child's tray and ask him to take that number of beads away on his tray. Use numbers that won't necessitate bead borrowing the first few times. For example, 365 − 241.

4) Place the number-symbol card representing the number the child has taken away under the large number-symbol cards.

5) Now count the remaining beads and place the appropriate small number-symbol cards under the other number-symbol cards to obtain the answer.

6) Repeat the process, using numbers where borrowing is necessary.

7) Let the children work alone.

PURPOSE:

To show the child that subtraction is the breaking up of a large number into smaller ones.

To show the working of the subtraction process.

DIVISION

Age 5½–8

MATERIAL:
All Golden Bead material.
One set of large number-symbol cards.
Several sets of small number-symbol cards.
Several trays.

DEMONSTRATION:

1) Place a number, e.g., 4862 of beads and the corresponding large number-symbol cards on the table.

2) To divide the quantity by two you must have two children, each with a tray, come to the table, or use two markers to represent two children.

3) Explain that you are going to divide the beads among the children so that they will each receive the same amount.

4) Always begin with a number that can be divided evenly.

5) Beginning with the thousand-cubes, give one to the first child, one to the second, then another to the first and another to the second. Do the same with the hundreds, tens and units until the beads have been divided evenly among the two children.

6) Check the two trays to be sure that both children have received the same number of beads.

7) Beginning with the thousands, count the beads, changing where necessary, and give the child the number from the small number-symbol cards.

8) Explain to the children that you will only need the beads and number from one of them. Remove the small number-symbol cards from one tray and show them, as you place them under the large number, that 4862 divided by 2 equals 2431.

9) Continue in this manner, always using the exact number of children (or trays) that the number is to be divided by. Begin with simple problems and work up to more difficult ones, using larger dividers and involving more changing and remainders.

PURPOSE: To show how division is done.
To illustrate the breaking up of a large quantity into a smaller one.

THE SEGUIN BOARDS
THE NUMBERS 11–19

Age 4½–6

MATERIAL EXERCISE I:	9 ten-bars. The short bead stair (1-9). Small cloth mat for table.
DEMONSTRATION:	1) Take 3 ten-bars and the short beads 1 to 3 to the child's table. 2) Lay a ten-bar on the table, place a unit-bead next to it, and explain that this is how you make eleven. 3) Continue in this way through thirteen, using the Three-Period Lesson. 4) When the child understands the procedure, continue with the remaining beads to introduce the quantities eleven through nineteen.
PURPOSE:	To learn the names and sequence of the numbers 11 to 19. To associate names with quantities.

MATERIAL EXERCISE II:	The Seguin teen board, with number cards 1 to 9.
DEMONSTRATION:	1) Take the short Seguin board and number cards 1 to 4 to the child's table.

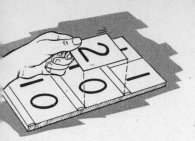

2) Place the 1 card over the zero on the first 10 and say, "This is how we make eleven."

3) Continue in this way with the cards through 4 (14), using the Three-Period Lesson.

4) Introduce the other board and the remaining number cards in the same manner through nineteen.

PURPOSE:

To learn the sequence of the numbers 11 to 19.

To associate the quantity with the written number.

MATERIAL
EXERCISE III:

The Seguin teen board, with number cards 1 to 9.
9 ten-bars.
The short bead stair (1 to 9).

DEMONSTRATION:

1) Place the 1 number card over the zero of the first 10 and place a ten-bar and a unit-bead next to it, saying, "Eleven."

2) Proceed in this manner with the numbers through 19.

3) Review with the child by asking him to place a certain number and quantity ("Show me fifteen," "Show me twelve," etc.).

PURPOSE:

To associate the numbers and quantities 11 to 19 and to understand their sequence.

THE NUMBERS 11–99

Age 5–6

MATERIAL EXERCISE I:	9 ten-bars. Small cloth mat for table.
DEMONSTRATION:	1) Take 6 ten-bars to the child's table. 2) Place 1 ten-bar in front of him and say, "Ten." 3) Take it away, replacing it with 2 ten-bars and say, "Twenty." 4) Proceed in this manner until he understands the numbers 10 through 30. 5) Use the Three-Period Lesson. 6) In the same way introduce the numbers through 90.
PURPOSE:	To learn the numbers 10 to 90 and their sequence. To introduce the conventional terms "ten, twenty, thirty," etc. (Up until now, they have been referred to as "two tens, three tens," etc.)

MATERIAL EXERCISE II:	The Seguin board (10 to 90).
DEMONSTRATION:	1) Point to the number 10, saying, "This is ten." 2) Introduce the first few numbers, 10, 20, 30, 40, 50, using the Three-Period Lesson.

3) Introduce the remaining numbers (60-90) and be certain that the child knows their names and recognizes them readily.

PURPOSE: To show how these numbers are written.

MATERIAL EXERCISE III: The Seguin boards (10 to 90).
9 ten-bars.

DEMONSTRATION:
1) Place a ten-bar by the number 10 on the Seguin board, saying, "Ten."
2) Place 2 ten-bars by the number 20, saying, "Twenty."
3) Introduce the first few numbers, 20, 30, 40, and their quantities, using the Three-Period Lesson.
4) Introduce the remaining numbers and quantities.
5) Review by clearing the ten-bars and asking the child, "Put out the beads for twenty," etc. Then reverse the procedure, handing the child a number of bars and saying, "Put those in the right place."

PURPOSE: To associate the written number and the quantity.

MATERIAL EXERCISE IV: The Seguin board (10 to 90), with number cards 1 to 9.
9 ten-bars.
9 unit-beads.

DEMONSTRATION:

1) Place the 1 card over the "0" of the 10, saying, "Eleven," and place a ten-bar and a bead next to it.
2) Remove the 1 card; replace it with a 2. Add a unit-bead and say, "Twelve."
3) Continue in this way through 19.
4) Explain to the child, "I have no more cards and no more single beads, so we must go to twenty."
5) Go through 20 to 29, 30 to 39, etc., through 99, using this same process, of placing and removing the cards and adding the beads.
6) The child can work alone through 99 after he understands the process.

PURPOSE:

To learn to count to 99 in sequence. To understand the written numbers and quantities through 99.

THE SNAKE GAME
Age 5½–7

MATERIAL: One or two sets of short bead stairs.
9 ten-bars.
One set of black and white bead bars.

DEMONSTRATION:
1) Lay the black and white beads in a triangle.
2) Make a "snake" by laying the colored beads of the short bead stair end to end in random order.
3) Begin counting the bead stairs at one end of the snake until ten is reached. Replace every ten beads with a ten-bar. When extra units of the bead stair must be eliminated, replace that number with the appropriate black and white bead bar.
4) Begin counting again after the ten-bar, starting with the number represented by the black and white bead bar and continuing until ten is reached. Again replace the colored beads with a ten-bar and hold the place of any extras with a black and white bead.
5) Continue counting in this way until the snake has been changed from colored beads to ten-bars.

Take for example:
$$6+2+8+7+1+9+3+5+4$$

Ten will be reached two into the eight-bar. Place a ten-bar, remove the six-, two- and eight-bar and hold the place of those remaining from the eight-bar with a black and white six bead bar. Begin counting again at the beginning of the black and white bar. Ten will be reached into the seven-bar. Remove the seven-bar, replace it with a ten-bar and a black three-bar, etc. The end result should be 45, or four ten-bars and a black five-bar.

6) To double-check your answer, sort out the colored beads that had formed the snake and place them together in tens (e.g., $8+2$, $9+1$, $7+3$, $6+4$, equaling 40 and a remainder of 5, or 45).

PURPOSE:
Preparation for learning addition tables.

A reiteration of the need to return each time to the 1-10 sequence in counting.

THE ADDITION BOARD
Age 5½–7

MATERIAL:	The addition strip board materials. Addition tables.
DEMONSTRATION:	1) Begin with any addition table; e.g., 8.
	2) Place the blue 8 ruler on the board; beside it, place the red 1 ruler.
	3) The result is 9, as read above; fill the answer in on the addition table.
	4) Remove the red 1 ruler. Replace it with the red 2 ruler and write the answer on the addition table.
	5) Continue until all the table is filled in. The child repeats all the tables in this manner.
	6) Let the child see how many ways he can form one number. For example, 8: First place the blue 1 ruler and the red 7 ruler; under this, place the blue 2 and the red 6; then the $3+5$, $4+4$, $5+3$, $6+2$, $7+1$ rulers. The child will see that after $4+4$, the combinations are repeated in reverse order.
	7) The child can check his answers against the summary of addition tables.
PURPOSE:	To establish a systematic way for learning the addition tables.

THE ADDITION CHART
Age 5½–7

MATERIAL:	Addition chart with answers filled in. The combinations of addition tables from $1+1=$ to $9+9=$.
DEMONSTRATION:	1) Place the materials on the table. Let the child look at the chart.
	2) The child takes a combination slip. For example, $4+7=$.
	3) Place one finger on the printed 4 to the left of the chart.
	4) With the right hand, place a finger on the 7 to the right of the chart.
	5) Move fingers across and down until they meet at 11.
	6) The child writes $4+7=11$. (This should be done on the square ruled paper, with each number in a separate square.)
	7) This procedure is repeated as more slips are drawn; the answer is found and the result written down.
PURPOSE:	The learning and memorizing of the addition tables.

THE BLANK ADDITION CHART
Age 5½–7

MATERIAL: The blank addition chart.
Combinations of addition tables from
$1 + 1 =$ to $9 + 9 =$, and separate
answer slips.

DEMONSTRATION:
1) Use the same procedure as in the previous Addition Chart lesson.

2) The child draws a slip with a combination on it.

3) From memory, he thinks of the answer and finds the appropriate slip.

4) The answer slip is placed on the blank addition chart in the proper square.

5) The child continues in this way until all the squares are filled.

6) The child may check his work against the Addition Chart, which has the answers filled in.

7) The combinations may also be written on paper as the child goes along.

PURPOSE: The final test for checking the child's memory of the addition tables.

THE ADDITION TABLES
Age 5½–7

MATERIAL:	1 short bead stair. Combinations of addition tables from $1+1=$ to $9+9=$ without answers.

DEMONSTRATION:

1) Set the materials on the table; the child is usually able to do this exercise without the aid of the teacher.

2) The child picks a table, e.g., 2.

3) The first combination is $2+1=$.

4) A two-bar and a one-bar are placed next to each other.

5) The beads are counted and the result (3) is seen and recorded on the table.

6) The bead bars are replaced in the box.

7) The child continues in this manner until $2+9=11$ is done. He then repeats the process with the other addition tables.

PURPOSE: To reinforce the addition tables.

THE MULTIPLICATION BOARD
Age 6–9

MATERIAL:	Multiplication Board materials. Multiplication sum cards. Multiplication Summary Chart.
DEMONSTRATION:	1) Choose a multiplication table to work with, e.g., 3.
	2) Place the small 3-card in the slot at the left-hand side of the board.
	3) The first problem will be 3×1.
	4) Place the counter above the 1 at the top of the board, and place three beads in a row underneath it. Count and write the answer.
	5) Next, to find 3×2, he moves the counter to above the 2 and places another row of three beads under the 2, counts that there are six beads, and writes it on the paper.
	6) Continue in this way with each table, not necessarily going in sequence, but always completing the table chosen.
	7) Answers may be checked against the Multiplication Summary Chart.
PURPOSE:	To learn the multiplication tables in a systematic way.

THE MULTIPLICATION CHARTS
Age 6–9

MATERIAL:	The Multiplication Summary Chart.
	A box of slips with the multiplication combinations of the tables 2 to 10. Pencil and paper.
DEMONSTRATION:	1) The child draws a slip from the box, e.g., $6 \times 4 =$.
	2) Find the 6 at the left-hand side of the summary chart and the 4 at the top, run fingers down and across until they meet at 24.
	3) Write down the sums and the answers as each is found.
	4) Continue in this way with all the slips containing the combinations.
PURPOSE:	To memorize the multiplication tables.

THE BLANK
MULTIPLICATION CHART
Age 6–9

MATERIAL:

The blank multiplication chart.
Slips with the multiplication combinations of the tables 2-10.
Answer slips.
Pencil and paper.

DEMONSTRATION:

1) The child draws a combination slip.
2) From memory he knows the answer, so he finds the answer slip and places it in the appropriate square of the blank Multiplication Chart.
3) The answer may also be written on a sheet of paper.
4) Continue in this way with all the multiplication tables until the chart is filled.
5) Answers may be checked against the Multiplication Summary Chart if necessary, but by now the child should have memorized the tables.
6) Small individual charts may also be used to fill in answers to a specific table.

PURPOSE:

To test the child's memory of the multiplication tables.

THE SUBTRACTION STRIP BOARD

Age 6–9

MATERIAL:
The subtraction strip board materials.
Summary of subtraction tables.
Blank subtraction tables for the child to fill in.

DEMONSTRATION:
1) The child takes one of the subtraction tables, e.g., 5.
2) For the problem 5 − 3, place the white ruler on the strip board, covering all the numbers to the right of the 5.
3) Place the blue 3 ruler to the left of the white ruler and next to it; the answer will show as 2.
4) The child records the answer and may check his answer with the completed table summary.
5) Continue in this way until the tables are finished, always using the white ruler to show the minuend (the larger number).

PURPOSE:
To acquaint the child with a systematic working of the subtraction table.

THE SUBTRACTION
SUMMARY CHART
Age 6–9

MATERIAL: The Subtraction Summary Chart.
Slips of paper with the subtraction
table combinations.
Paper and pencil.

DEMONSTRATION: 1) Show the child how to use the
subtraction chart by finding the
first and larger number at the top
or left hand side of the chart and
the second and lower number at
the right.
2) A slip is taken from the box,
e.g. 6 – 2 = .
3) Place the left finger on 6 and the
right finger on 2; move down and
across to 4.
4) Write on your paper 6 – 2 = 4.
5) Continue in this way with the
other number combinations.

PURPOSE: To learn the positive results of the
subtraction combinations from 1 to
18.

THE BLANK SUBTRACTION CHART
Age 6–9

MATERIAL:	The blank subtraction chart. Subtraction table combinations and answer slips.
DEMONSTRATION:	1) Use the same procedure as in the previous Subtraction Summary Chart exercise.
	2) Draw a slip with a combination on it.
	3) From memory find the answer slip.
	4) Place the appropriate answer slip in the correct box on the blank subtraction chart.
	5) Continue in this way until the blank chart is filled with answer slips.
	6) Answers may be checked against the completed subtraction summary chart.
	7) The combinations may also be written on paper.
PURPOSE:	The final test for checking the child's memory of the subtraction tables.

THE SHORT BEAD STAIR
ADDITION AND SUBTRACTION
Age 6–8

MATERIAL:
1 short bead stair.
Pencil and paper.

DEMONSTRATION:

1) Place the one bead next to the two-bar, and the three-bar parallel to them.

2) Count the beads, and show that 1 and 2 are the same as 3.

3) Use 1 unit-bead with each bar, one at a time, showing the addition process.

4) Use the same procedure with the two-bar, three-bar, etc.

5) Find all the combinations that make 10, that make 9, etc.

6) Let the child continue on his own.

7) Use ¾"-square ruled paper for the child to write the sums as he goes along.

Each number or symbol should be written centered in its own square.

8) At first the child should write on the line, skipping a row in between his problems to make them easier to read,

e.g., $4 + 3 = 7$

$2|+|6|=|8$

Later they may be written,

$$\begin{array}{r} 4 \\ +\,3 \\ \hline 7 \end{array}$$

9) Sum books may also be used, enabling the child to see the problem, find the answer with the bead stair, and write it down.

10) When the child has become adept with the addition of the beads, use the same procedure (reversed) to teach subtraction.

PURPOSE: To reinforce the child's knowledge of addition and subtraction.

THE SHORT BEAD STAIR
MULTIPLICATION
Age 7–9

MATERIAL:

10 sets of short bead stairs.

10 ten-bars.

Multiplication sum cards.

Multiplication Summary Chart.

DEMONSTRATION:

1) The child chooses any multiplication sum cards he wants to work with, e.g. 3.

2) He must begin with the $3 \times 1 =$, so he places a three-bar on the table.

3) Next is $3 \times 2 =$, so he places another three-bar next to it, counts the beads and writes down the answer.

4) The child continues in this way to $3 \times 10 =$, checking his answers against the Multiplication Summary Chart.

5) All the tables through 10 are worked in this way.

6) If the child wants to work the 11 tables, use a ten-bar with 1 unit-bead and continue in the same way. The 12 tables are worked with a ten-bar and two-bar, etc.

PURPOSE:

To learn a systematic way for working the multiplication tables.

THE DIVISION CHART
Age 7–9

MATERIAL:	Division Summary Chart. Division sum cards.
DEMONSTRATION:	1) Take a sum card.
	2) Show the child how to find the answer on the summary chart.
	3) For example, if the problem is $28 \div 4 =$, he should place one finger on the 28 at the top of the chart, the other finger on 4 at the left of the chart and move the fingers down and across until they meet on the answer, which is 7.
	4) The child will write the answer on his paper and continue to work all the division problems in this way.
PURPOSE:	To learn the division tables.

THE BLANK DIVISION CHART

Age 7–9

MATERIAL:	Blank division chart. Division sum cards. Answer slips.
DEMONSTRATION:	1) Place the material to the table.
	2) The child takes a slip from the combinations box, e.g., $12 \div 3 =$.
	3) He remembers the answer, 4, from memory and looks in the answer box for the slip with 4 on it.
	4) By moving his fingers across and down the blank chart he finds the appropriate answer square and places the 4 in it, or the child can write in the answer on the blank chart.
	5) The child may test his answers against the Division Summary Chart.
PURPOSE:	To test the child's memory of the division tables.

THE DIVISION BOARD

Age 7–9

MATERIAL: The short-division board material.
81 green pegs.
9 green markers.
Division tables to work.
Paper and pencil.

DEMONSTRATION:

1) Place any number of pegs up to 81 in the lid of the peg box, e.g., 27.

2) Write the number 27 on a piece of paper.

3) The first problem will be $27 \div 9 =$.

4) As the number must be divided by 9, place nine markers at the top of the board.

5) Placing the pegs across the board, give each marker the same number of pegs.

6) When the problem is completed, each marker will have three pegs, and the answer is written on the paper.

7) The next problem is $27 \div 8 =$, so remove onc marker and begin dividing the pegs among them. There will be three pegs left over, so write $27 \div 8 = 3$ (rem. 3) .

8) The child continues working tables in this way, becoming familiar with the board and the division process.

PURPOSE: To learn to work and understand the division tables.

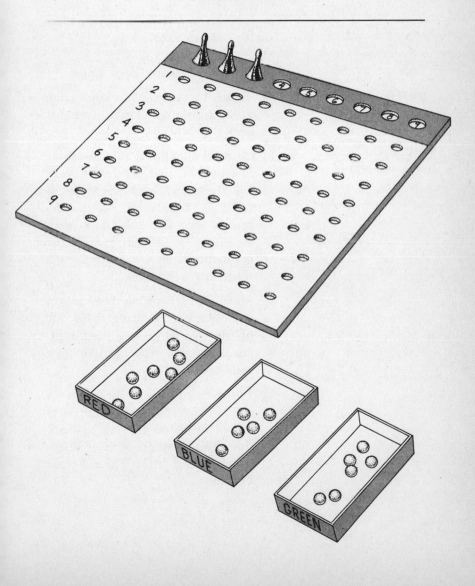

THE SHORT BEAD FRAME
INTRODUCTION
Age 7–9

MATERIAL:

Golden Bead material.
Short bead frame.
Ruled paper with colored lines.

DEMONSTRATION:

1) Bring to the table a thousand-cube, a hundred-square, a ten-bar and a unit-bead.

2) Show the child the bead frame and explain that the green beads on the right each represent a unit; the blue beads each represent a ten; the red beads each represent a hundred and the green beads on the far left each represent a thousand.

3) Show that ten of any bead group can always be exchanged for one of the following (e.g., ten unit-beads can be exchanged for one ten-bar).

4) Let the child count the beads on the bar; then move a specific number of beads on the bar and ask the child how many it is. Continue using the Three-Period Lesson.

5) The bead frame may be used working across or up and down. As the child will be working with ruled paper with lines going top to bottom, it seems easier to use the frame in the same manner.

6) Show the child how to move the beads to make the combinations. Write the numbers represented by the beads on the corresponding line of his paper.

PURPOSE: To familiarize the child with the operation of the short bead frame, preparatory to addition, subtraction and multiplication.

THE SHORT BEAD FRAME
ADDITION

Age 7–9

MATERIAL:

Short bead frame.
Ruled paper with colored lines.

DEMONSTRATION:

1) Write a sum that doesn't involve carrying on the colored lines, e.g.,

$$2431$$
$$+3215$$

2) The child moves the beads down the wire, each in turn to find his answer, which he then records on the paper.

3) Example: There will be 6 on the unit wire, 4 on the ten wire, 6 on the hundred wire and 5 on the thousands. Thus the answer is 5646.

4) Later give sums that involve carrying, e.g.,

$$3455$$
$$+1267$$

5) Move the five unit-beads down; next you must move seven, but you only have five. Move the five down and exchange the unit beads for one blue ten-bead. Push the ten green beads up and bring two down (the remaining two from the seven). Count five ten beads

and bring them down. Count the remaining four more and exchange for ten; bring the remaining two beads down. Count four red beads down, then bring two more down. Bring three beads down for the thousands, and bring one down. At the bottom of the frame will be two unit-beads, two tens, seven hundreds and four thousands, or 4722, which is your answer.

6) The child writes the problem as he goes along, noting the carrying on his paper as well as on the frame.

PURPOSE: To learn addition.

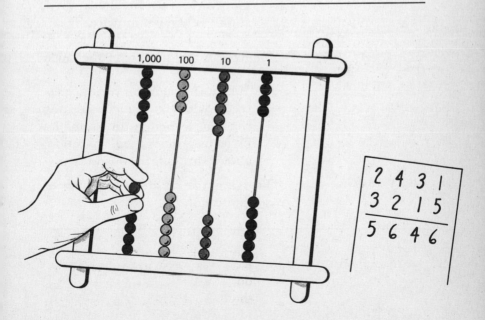

THE SHORT BEAD FRAME
MULTIPLICATION

Age 7–9

MATERIAL:

Short bead frame.
Ruled paper with colored lines.

DEMONSTRATION:

1) On the lined paper, write an example that doesn't need changing, e.g.,

$$3214$$
$$\underline{\times 2}$$

2) On the unit wire of the frame, move four beads twice; move one ten twice; two hundreds twice and three thousands twice. Total: 6428.

3) Record the answer on the ruled paper.

4) When the child is ready, proceed with examples needing changing; then with examples involving more multiplication, always changing, as in addition.

PURPOSE:

To teach the child the working of multiplication.

THE SHORT BEAD FRAME
SUBTRACTION
Age 7–9

MATERIAL: Short bead frame.
Ruled paper with colored lines.

DEMONSTRATION:
1) On the ruled paper, write a sum that doesn't need changing, e.g.

$$6219$$
$$-2201$$

2) Arrange the number 6219 on the top of the frame, and beginning with the unit-beads, take away 2201. The answer will be 4018. Record the answer on ruled paper.

3) After several simpler sums, use one involving changing, e.g.,

$$3654$$
$$-1365$$

4) Arrange the number 3654 on the bottom of the frame. You cannot take five beads from four, so borrow from the tens. (Take one bead away from the tens, leaving four, and replace the ten unit-beads at the bottom of the wire, taking away one, etc.) Record the answer on ruled paper.

5) Give more difficult sums as the child is ready for them.

PURPOSE: To learn the working of subtraction.

SHORT DIVISION

Age 7–9

MATERIAL: The short-division board materials. Ruled paper with colored lines.

DEMONSTRATION:

1) Explain the value of the pegs; the green pegs are worth one each, each blue peg is worth ten, each red peg is worth a hundred, each green peg is worth a thousand.

2) Show the child how to write the sum step by step as he goes along.

3) Give the child a problem to work, e.g., $6339 \div 3 =$.

4) As the sum will be divided by 3, place three markers in the first three places at the top of the board.

5) Count six green pegs into the lid of the first box (6000) ; in the lid of the red box, place three red pegs (300) ; in the lid of the blue box place three blue pegs (30) ;

and in the lid of the green box place nine green pegs (9) .

6) Beginning with the green pegs representing thousands, the pegs must be divided evenly between the three markers.

7) Place all the peg boxes to the right of the board.

8) Bring the box of green thousand pegs and place it above the board to the left and divide the six pegs evenly among the three markers; each has received two, so write 2 on the paper.

9) Clear the board and return the box of green pegs to the right. Bring the box of red pegs and place it at the top of the board, proceeding as before.

10) Continue in this way until the answer to the problem is found.

11) Begin with simple problems, working up to more difficult ones involving carrying.

12) As each problem is worked, the answer is recorded, first on the ruled paper and then on regular paper.

13) The division problem is worked out completely on the paper showing the changing and any remainders.

PURPOSE: To understand the working of short division.

FRACTIONS

Age 5–7

MATERIAL:

The fraction insets.
Fraction cards.
Fraction booklets.

DEMONSTRATION EXERCISE I:

1) Bring only the fractional insets and frames for whole, half, third and fourth to the table.

2) Place the representative portion from each of the insets on the table, and use the Three Period Lesson to introduce the portions and their names to the child.

3) When the child understands the portion and associates it with its name, show how the parts of the frame combine to make a whole, e.g., three thirds, four fourths, etc.

4) Show how the pieces can be interchanged, e.g. half may also be made of two $\frac{1}{4}$ pieces, etc.

5) Introduce the remaining fraction frames in the same way.

PURPOSE:

To show that a whole is made up of fractional parts.

EXERCISE II:

1) Show the child how the fractions are written, e.g., "half" can also be written "½," etc.

2) Bring out the fraction cards for each set of fractions and place them on the fractional pieces. Use the Three-Period Lesson.

3) Teach the names *numerator* and *denominator,* explaining that the numerator tells how many and the denominator names the fraction.

4) Let the children exchange various fractional pieces ("Let's see if we can make a half out of any others," etc.) .

5) Show how individual pieces of a whole can be grouped to form a larger part of the whole, and place the fraction card for combinations on the area.

6) Do many substitutions, etc., to gain a good working knowledge of the fractions and how they are formed and how they combine.

7) Always have an empty frame handy to work your fraction problems in, as it makes it easier for the child to see the makeup.

PURPOSE:

To familiarize the child with the fractions.

REDUCTION OF FRACTIONS
Age 7–10

MATERIAL:	The fraction insets. Booklet of fractions to be reduced.
DEMONSTRATION:	1) Remove one half of the fraction from the circle and ask the child if he can fit pieces from other fractional insets into the space. As he does this, he will see that the half cannot be filled with thirds, but two fourths fill the space exactly. He continues working in this way to see which other fractions fill the half space and records his results, e.g., $1/2 = 2/4 = 3/6 = 4/8 = 5/10$.
	2) Continue in this way with other fractions (third, fourth, etc.) until the child becomes familiar with the various substitutions.
	3) Give the child a small booklet with one fraction on each page that can be reduced.
	4) If the example is 4/10, explain that you want to change this for another equal fraction with as few parts as possible, etc.

5) When the child has used the material for some time and understands it, explain the rules for reduction of fractions; and show how the answer can be reduced to its lowest common denominator.

PURPOSE: To understand the fractions and their component parts.

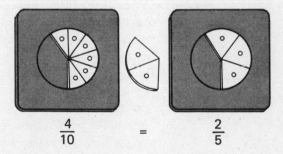

$$\frac{4}{10} \quad = \quad \frac{2}{5}$$

ADDITION OF FRACTIONS

Age 7–10

MATERIAL:

The fraction insets.

Fraction booklets for addition problems having the same denominator.

DEMONSTRATION:

1) Use an empty frame to work the problems in.

2) The child takes the booklet, reads the first problem and by working with the appropriate insets, finds the answer and writes it down.

3) For example, if the problem is $2/3 + 1/3 =$, he places two thirds in his empty frame, then adds another third and sees that $2/3 + 1/3 = 3/3 = 1$.

4) When the child has had some practice with this, explain that when fractions have the same denominator, only the numerators should be added and the answer reduced to the lowest common denominator.

5) Eventually, the child can work the problems out on paper without using the materials.

PURPOSE:

To acquaint the child with addition of fractions.

MULTIPLICATION OF FRACTIONS
Age 7–10

MATERIAL:

The fraction insets.
Fraction booklets for multiplication.

DEMONSTRATION:

1) The child reads the first problem in the booklet; if it is $\frac{1}{4} \times 3 =$, he places $\frac{1}{4}$ into the frame three times to find his answer.

2) Explain that you multiply the numerator by the whole number and reduce to the lowest common denominator if necessary.

PURPOSE:

To acquaint the child with the multiplication of fractions.

SUBTRACTION OF FRACTIONS
Age 7½–10

MATERIAL:
The fraction insets.
Fraction booklets for subtraction problems having the same denominator.

DEMONSTRATION:
1) If the problem is $3/4 - 2/4 =$, the child will place $3/4$ in the empty frame and then remove $2/4$, seeing that only $1/4$ remains.

2) He writes, $3/4 - 2/4 = 1/4$.

3) As in addition, explain to the child that one numerator is subtracted from the other and the answer is reduced if necessary.

PURPOSE:
To acquaint the child with the subtraction of fractions.

DIVISION OF FRACTIONS
Age 8–10

MATERIAL:

The fraction insets.
Fraction booklets for division.
Markers.

DEMONSTRATION:

1) Always divide by whole numbers.

2) If the problem is $6/7 \div 3 =$, take out six sevenths. Take three markers to represent the divisor and divide the six sevenths among the markers.

3) He sees that the answer is $2/7$, and writes this down.

4) In a problem such as $1/2 \div 3 =$, the half cannot be divided, so exchange it for three sixths and continue the problem.

5) Explain that you divide the numerator by the whole number, and if this is not possible, multiply the denominator by the whole number.

PURPOSE:

To acquaint the child with division of fractions.

LOWEST COMMON MULTIPLE
Age 6–8

MATERIAL:	Factor and multiple board.
DEMONSTRATION:	1) Begin with the number two.
	2) Using two differently colored sets of pegs, arrange the pegs in a straight row, alternating the colors to show the multiples.
	3) For example: two red, two yellow, two red, two yellow, etc.
	4) Show the child how to count them, "One, *two,* three, *four,*" and so on.
	5) Then show him how to count them in multiples of two, "Two, four, six," etc.
	6) The multiples of any small numbers can be found in this way.
	7) One day let the child set out the multiples of several different numbers on the board, to find the common multiples (e.g., 3, 6, 9, 12 are multiples of 3).
PURPOSE:	To understand the meaning of multiples.

FACTORS ON THE PEGBOARD
Age 6–8

MATERIAL: Large pegboard with 30 rows of 30 holes.
Boxes of colored pegs.

DEMONSTRATION:
1) Explain that a factor is a number that goes evenly into another number.
2) The child chooses a number under 30, e.g., 10.
3) He places ten pegs in the lids of several boxes, using a different color for each ten.
4) First, he tries to arrange the ten pegs in twos on the board, from top to bottom. He can, and finds that 2 is a factor of 10.
5) Leaving those pegs on the board, he chooses ten pegs of another color and tries to arrange them in threes under the twos. This isn't possible, so he goes on to four, etc.
6) Only the multiples that can be factored (or divided evenly) are left on the board.
7) The child continues in this way and then records the factors of the given number on paper.
8) When he becomes familiar with this process, he can choose any two numbers under 30 and work

them at either side of the peg-board, finding their common factors and highest and lowest common factors, etc. (e.g., common factors of 12 and 18 are 2, 3, and 6; the highest common factor of 10 and 30 is 10; the lowest common factor of 10 and 30 is 2).

PURPOSE:

To understand the terms and to find the factors of various numbers.

FACTORS AND MULTIPLES
Age 6½–8

MATERIAL:	A chart with numbers through 100. Colored pencils.
DEMONSTRATION:	1) Give the child a chart and explain that you are going to find all the multiples of 2. This means all the numbers into which two will divide exactly.
	2) Begin with the 1, and count "One, two"; draw a ring around 2 with the colored pencil. Count "One, two" again and draw a ring around 4. Continue until 100 is reached.
	3) Let the child use this same procedure to find other multiples.
	4) Let the child find the multiples of any two numbers on the chart using a differently colored pencil for each of the two.
	5) Then let him look for numbers with two rings around them; explain that those are multiples of both numbers.
	6) He can look for the lowest common multiple of two numbers, the highest, etc.
PURPOSE:	To learn and understand the meanings of the terms. An introduction to finding multiples and factors.

□

Language Development

INTRODUCTION

The learning of language is truly the child's most remarkable intellectual achievement, and yet it is rapidly accomplished in a very short time span. Ideally the parents, who are the child's first language teachers, should begin during the early infancy of the child to give verbal meaning to the things in his environment. Sadly, many parents today fail to spend enough time talking to their babies, because they underestimate the important role the human voice plays in the intellectual development of the young. Admittedly, you sometimes feel a bit self-conscious rambling on at great length to a three-month-old infant, and yet this is where it all begins, as language patterns are slowly and gradually built up. The following synopsis of language development in the small child shows how much is learned and absorbed in the first two years.

0-3 months	watches lips move
6 months	repeats syllables (babbles)
9 months	words have meaning
12 months	intentional and conscious repeating of words
15 months	objects have names
18 months	baby talk begins, words
21 months	phrases
24 months	sentences, syntax

The child's success in school can be largely determined by what has been done in the home to give him the background for language development. Many varied language experiences are necessary to build and enrich the child's foundation for learning to read and write.

Encourage your preschool child's curiosity by answering his seemingly unending questions, and give him every opportunity to develop and strengthen language skills by talking to him. Always speak distinctly and use clear and accurate pronunciation. Remember that this is a stage when much is learned by imitation and both good and bad language habits will be readily copied. Teach the correct names of people, places and objects. Try to avoid baby talk. Don't be afraid of introducing large or unfamiliar words, for this is how children learn them. The young child loves to talk about parallelograms, rhododendrons, cumulus clouds and so on. In fact, I remember one three-year-old I taught in school who knew all of the dinosaur names and pronounced them with no difficulty at all. Give names and meanings to everything in the child's environment, and talk to him about numbers, colors, etc. ("Let's wear your red coat today," "Please put the vase in the center of the table," "One, two, three buttons").

Encourage your child to talk with other children and adults. Take him places. Expose him to many different experiences and situations to stimulate his interest and conversation. Ask the child to tell you about his experiences and write them down. Then read them back to him so that he begins to develop a concept of the printed word. The preschooler usually has an enthusiastic interest in being read to and having books of his own to "read." Take the time to read to your child, letting him sit so that he is able to watch your lips move and see your eyes move from left to right. This will also help to develop and increase his attention span, so necessary for later reading. Simple nursery rhymes, songs, stories and picture books that stimulate the child's imagination and lead to conversation are good choices at this time. Introduce your child to the local children's library and help him gain an interest in borrowing books. Records are also good sources of vocabulary building and give the child opportunity for hearing and mimicking pronunciation. Most important, show an interest in what your child says and does, and *listen* to him. Nothing dims a child's enthusiasm faster than sensing that his parents aren't really interested and are just going through the motions.

Reading is the most important fundamental skill your child will ever learn. Reading means success. In school, in work, and in life. Without a good reading background a child is virtually doomed, for it is on this that the major portion of his future learning and success depends. Educators and psychologists alike agree that the child who cannot read is practically uneducable, and if he isn't reading well by age eight or nine the chances are slim that he will ever become even a fair reader. It is a sad fact that children who cannot read tend to become the greatest disciplinary problem in schools today. Their frustrations reach a peak when they find that their means for understanding and expressing themselves are wholly inadequate, and they ultimately reject school and the whole learning process. If your child is unhappy with school and seems to be lagging behind, look first to his reading habits—herein usually lies the clue.

Statistics on nonreaders and poor readers in the elementary grades and even on the high school level are frighteningly high. The standardized tests of the 1920's were the first real indication that a large percentage of first-graders were failing to learn to read adequately. With this fact established, the next question was, Why? Bad teaching methods were the first problem, and lack of interest and stimulation at home was another. Controversies began, which still rage today, as to which method of reading was best: phonetic, look-say, sight, oral, silent. Throughout the endless debates the merits of phonetic reading for the young child have continued to be recognized, because phonics is a logical method—the connection between sounds and writing make it possible to turn sounds into written words, thereby teaching the child to think rather than simply guess. Phonics is truly the key that unlocks the door to reading for the young child, for if he learns to read phonetically he can read everything and anything with ease.

Years ago the common misconception was that children were not mentally ready to read until at least age six, and parents were repeatedly warned that under no circumstances should they attempt to teach their youngsters to read before this time. Fortunately this idea has now been dispelled, but not before the spontaneous introduction to reading of many children had been unwittingly thwarted. Today there is common agreement that preschoolers not only *can* be taught to read but that this is the peak time they naturally and enthusiastically absorb reading skills. Young children have been found to be so eager that given the slightest encouragement they can almost teach themselves. In fact, once a child realizes the magic of letters and words his enthusiasm and curiosity are insatiable. Thanks to the marvelous background that our preschoolers have today through mass visual-auditory media, teaching them to read is usually extremely successful at an early age.

Reading is not nearly so complex a process as it is made out to be, and parents shouldn't be leery of teaching their children the fundamentals before they enter school. A good teacher will welcome this readiness background in your child. Only a teacher who is unsure of herself will feel threatened by a child in kindergarten or first-grader who has already been introduced to reading and writing.

Visual perception and discrimination can be taught in many ways at home. Have your child look for pictures in magazines with various letter sounds in them. Let him make scrapbooks and make up his own stories to go with pictures. Encourage him to think and to become aware, visually and orally. Phonics at this stage is very much a game, and much repetition is essential for gradual but solid learning. Parents have found it both gratifying and easy to teach the basic letter sounds that enable their children to take their first step toward reading. Nothing is more exciting than to watch and be a part of your child's introduction to reading. The wide grin and bright-eyed look of pride and accomplishment as your child reads his first words are enough encouragement for any parent. Children seem to sense immediately that once they can put sounds together and form words there's truly nothing that they can't do. Many experts believe that the child who has learned to read before first grade has a decided advantage which he maintains throughout his school career. Furthermore, early reading at a time when it is most natural and gradual prevents the pressures and anxieties of competition of a later period in school, when the child *must* learn to read.

Don't hurry reading. When the child is ready you'll know, and as with talking, once he has learned to read there's no stopping him. The ideal age to teach reading is from four and a half to six. This is the time to simply transfer the interest in the spoken word to an interest in the written. It must be remembered that reading is largely a sensory matter; to be a good reader, the child must learn to discriminate between the different letter sounds and to match those sounds to the written letters. Reading is, after all, the translating of symbols and sounds into meanings. The more you expose your child to the printed word, the more anxious he will be to learn it.

Reading should be an easy and natural process. Repetition is the key word; be thorough and unhurried in your teaching. Give the child easy books so that he won't become discouraged, and by feeling successful his interest will continue to be aroused. Always maintain a positive approach, and share your child's enthusiasm for the exciting new world that is opening up for him. Have him read aloud to you or other members of the family to practice expression and good intonation. As the child becomes more adept at reading, he will often choose books which you think are too advanced. Don't discourage this, for he will learn much in this way. If he comes across unfamiliar words often enough, he will soon figure out their meanings by the context in which they are used. Around age seven, teach the child how to use the dictionary to look up words, their meanings and derivations. Many children will spend hours fascinated by dictionary reading.

Reading and writing are intertwined, with writing usually preceding actual reading. It was the spontaneous writing of the four-year-olds in the first Casa dei Bambini that first drew world attention to Dr. Montessori and her work. This "explosion into writing" was considered a phenomenon at a time when most children had no familiarity with the alphabet until age seven or eight. This, of course, was not something that occurred simply out of the blue. Through gradual work with the early sensorial materials, the children had prepared mind, eye and hand for this exciting adventure. Small-muscle control and eye-hand control and coordination had been developed and refined, along with the sharpening of the senses. Through the grasping of the knobbed materials with the thumb and first two fingers and working with the geometric insets, the child's hand was ready to hold and maneuver a pencil with ease. The sandpaper letters had enabled the child to feel the shapes of the letters and to trace the direction they would be written. Language development had added impetus to the young child's growing fascination with words. More important, through the early practical-life and sensorial exercises, the child had developed self-discipline, self-mastery and a spontaneous joy of learning and discovering new things. There had been no laborious writing drills and no specific lessons involving only writing.

Many youngsters, once they have learned to use a pencil, will spend hours copying words from cereal boxes, magazines, anything they can lay their hands on. Encourage this, for good writing comes with practice. Give the child ruled paper (lines spaced about three-quarters of an inch) and sharpened pencils—pencils of regular size, not the oversized pencils so often found in kindergartens or preschools. Write down new words that your child is curious about; write words for him to copy. As the child becomes more familiar with the letter sounds, write short notes to him and he'll soon be writing them to you. As his ability develops, encourage him to write letters to friends or grandparents and to write short stories on topics of his own choosing. Don't worry about good spelling; this will come in time, and it's more important for a child to write freely and spontaneously without feeling hampered. I've always given my children a diary for their fifth Christmas. This gift not only gives them incentive to write but also gives them the opportunity to sit down and reflect on what they have done during the day. Give your child the materials necessary for writing and then let him proceed at his own pace.

Encourage him, but don't rush him. Help him, but don't hinder him.

The proper formation of the letters is extremely important, and this will come naturally if the sandpaper letters have been properly taught. Some children tend to write in small, tight letters, while others will use large, sprawling ones. Strive for a happy medium, but don't discourage the child in doing so. Ruled paper is a subtle guide for good writing habits if you explain to the child how certain parts of the letters should touch the lines.

The Montessori language materials on the following pages should come only after the child has had experience with the sandpaper letters and is familiar with all of the alphabet sounds. The movable alphabet is the first step in word building. Familiar objects are used, and as the child says their names slowly, he listens for each letter sound, finds the letters and forms the words. Spelling is not important at this point. As the child sounds out each letter, encourage him to run the individual sounds together smoothly so that he can hear the word as a whole. This takes practice. The three- and four-letter "phonetic" words (words with vowels and consonants pronounced regularly) are used at first, then longer words are added. This word-building process will continue for some time and the child will think of it as a fascinating game.

Through the handling of the movable alphabet, the child is gaining invaluable preparation for writing, reading and spelling. He is becoming familiar with the alphabet and the way letters are blended to form words, as well as unconsciously understanding the analysis of words. Gradually he sees that the words all seem to need at least one blue letter (vowel). Soon the child can think up his own words, sound them out and "write" them with the movable alphabet. Often at this stage, after the child has formed the words on the mat, he will take pencil and paper and write them. Then he will write phrases and sentences. Once he has practiced composing and writing words in this way, he is ready and able to begin actual reading, as reading comes about by fully understanding words already constructed.

The two small, colored movable alphabets are introduced with the small digraph booklets to familiarize the child with sounds that usually come together in a word. You will notice that in this work with the movable alphabets the hand is used while the child perceives visually. Gradually your child learns regular and irregular words through a variety of exercises. During this time he will also be reading at his own pace books of his own choosing. By having learned the phonetics of certain letter combinations, he needn't rely on memory, but rather can sound words out on his own. Actual reading usually comes before age six, but the time of the child's own readiness is far more important than his chronological age.

Grammar should be introduced parallel to the reading scheme. The child now has developed a strong feeling for words, and as his vocabulary increases, the use of the different parts of speech also becomes important. Grammar rules are not taught as such until age six and a half. The child is first given experiences that lead to understanding the function. The first parts of speech are introduced while the child learns to read simple words. Later, through use of the farm objects, the child, instead of working only with words, can actually see the materials that are the indirect preparation for sentence analysis and grammar.

In learning the various rules involved with reading and grammar, the child is slowly and sequentially taken from the abstract to the more concrete. As each part of speech has its own distinguishing color, the child learns to recognize and understand syntax by sight and practice rather than lengthy explanations and drilling of rules.

Having learned the basics of reading and writing, there is virtually nothing your child cannot learn and assimilate later. Without this basic knowledge, future learning and development will be badly hampered.

The Three-Period Lesson should be used in introducing the following exercises. Remember, too, that the child should be given ample opportunity to write words and sentences as he learns them. After building words with the movable alphabet or making sentences with the cards, writing materials should be made available for the child to use at will.

MATERIALS:

HOW TO MAKE THEM

MOVABLE ALPHABET:

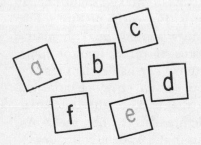

This alphabet is composed of individual alphabet letters usually cut from wood or heavy paper and about 1 to 1½" high. The consonants are red and the vowels blue.

For home use, six 1" squares should be cut for each lower-case alphabet letter. On these squares the letters can be written with felt pen, red for the consonants, blue for the vowels. These may be kept in a partitioned box of your own making. "Gem boxes" used by rock collectors can also be purchased for this purpose. For use with the digraphs you should also make two sets of alphabet cards, using two contrasting colors, and without differentiating the vowels and consonants.

OBJECT BOXES WITH NAME CARDS:

You should have separate boxes for three-letter words and words with four or more letters. The boxes should be distinguished in color (e.g., pink for the three-letter material, blue for the other material). Small objects identified by three- or four-letter "phonetic" words are included in the boxes. These objects (bag, belt, hat, pen, tag) can be found around the house. The name cards for these objects should be neatly printed on 2″ × 2½″ cards.

PICTURE CARDS:

Picture cards are made from construction paper and should be approximately 8½″ × 11″. On each sheet of paper stick six pictures. Make small name cards for each picture. The names should be "phonetic" words of three, four or more letters. The name cards may be kept in an envelope attached to the back of the particular picture sheet. (See the word lists in the Appendix for ideas.)

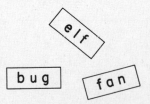

SENTENCE CARDS:

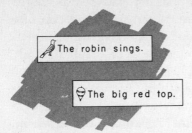

These cards are cut from construction paper and should be approximately 8″ × 2″. Paste a picture at the upper left-hand corner of each card. Neatly print a short descriptive phrase or sentence using "phonetic" words.

For example: The big red top.
                    The robin sings.
                    The hat is in the box.

Always begin the sentence with a capital letter and end it with a period.

PICTURE BOOKLETS:

Make, or have the child help you make, several small booklets, approximately 6″ × 8″, and not more than ten pages each. On each page (one side only) paste a picture. Underneath, neatly print a short sentence about the picture.

These booklets may be done in such a way that a story theme is used, or each page can represent an individual idea.

Note: Often pictures can be cut out of old workbooks or readers. Catalogs and magazines also are good sources.

DIGRAPH BOXES:

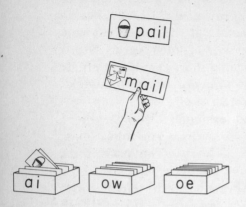

A digraph is a combination of two letters having a single sound. Find pictures of objects whose names have digraphs and mount them on small individual cards. Make word cards to go with the pictures. Have several pictures and words for each of the digraphs and keep them in individual boxes with the particular digraph printed on the front. You may keep them in envelopes instead of boxes. (See the word list in the Appendix for ideas.)

DIGRAPH BOOKLETS:

Individual booklets can be made for each of the digraphs. Each booklet should be approximately $3'' \times 1\frac{1}{2}''$ and not more than eight pages. The digraph is written on the front of the booklet, and each page (one side) has a word using that particular digraph. Write the digraph in a differently colored ink than the other letters.

DIGRAPH WORD LISTS:

ai	ow
pail	snow
train	low
snail	pillow
pain	blow
waist	slow

On sheets of paper approximately $11'' \times 4''$, write the digraph at the top, and list six or eight words using that digraph. The digraph should be written with ink or pencil of a contrasting color, and the words should be well spaced and neatly written on the papers.

PACKETS FOR DIGRAPHS:

Digraphs are kept together in an envelope. The letter combinations are printed on the front of the envelope. Inside is a card, approximately 3″ × 5″, for each digraph sound, listing several words in which it appears. Other packets are made for familiar letter combinations, such as *th* and *ch*, and the double letters at the ends of words, such as *ss*.

NOUN CARDS:

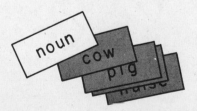

The noun cards are always black. Use a piece of black construction paper and divide it into thirty-six equal pieces, approximately 2⅛″ × 1¼″. Cut these pieces out. On each card write the name of an object in the house, using a white pen or pencil.

Make another set of cards like the above. On each card write the names of the members of your family or of the children in the classroom if you're in a school situation.

Make a third set of black noun cards to be used with the farm, zoo or whatever you have chosen.

A neutral-color card with "noun" written on it should be made for each separate group of cards.

THE FARM:

The farm is an example of a central idea with which specific objects can be associated. A replica of a barn can be made from a shoebox, and small toys related to farm life can be purchased (e.g., a farmer, hen, cow, hay, chicken, pig, horse, dog, etc.), or you can use pictures. Paste a picture of a barn on a large piece of green poster board. Cut out other pictures depicting farm animals and objects and glue them to individual pieces of cardboard. Because the farm is used in many of the exercises to teach the parts of speech, the word cards and other materials should relate to it.

SINGULAR AND PLURAL CARDS:

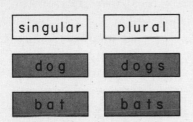

CARDS FOR GENDER:

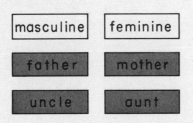

One of nine rules determines the formation of the plural of a word. These rules are explained in the exercise "Formation of the Plural" on page 136. Have nine small boxes or envelopes for each of these rules. Each box should contain two black packets of cards, one for the singular and one for the plural. (The packet of cards for the words made plural by adding *s* should be names of small movable objects in the room. See the word list in the Appendix for ideas for the other rules.) These cards are the same as the noun cards and should be separated by a neutral-colored card marked "singular" and "plural."

Gender cards are made the same way as the black noun cards. You should have three boxes, one for each rule. Each box will contain two sets of cards: one for the masculine nouns and one for their feminine equivalents. Two neutral-colored cards, marked "masculine" and "feminine" should be on top of each packet. (See the word list in the Appendix for ideas.)

ADJECTIVE CARDS:

The adjective cards are always royal blue. Make them in the same way as the noun cards, using blue paper and a white pen or pencil. A neutral-colored card marked "adjective" should be placed on top of the pile of cards. Write adjectives descriptive of farm animals (e.g., fat, big, strong).

Make twenty blue adjective cards and twenty black noun cards that could go together or be interchanged. Example:

adjective	noun
beautiful	dress
tall	tree
brown	house
little	boy

Make separate cards for the articles "the," "a," and "an."

adjective	noun
fat	dog
poisonous	snake
cool	water
square	box
juicy	orange

ADJECTIVE CARDS FOR DEGREE:

Three boxes or envelopes of cards representing the three rules (see page 142) for the degrees of adjectives should be made. Each box contains three sets of blue cards, with neutral-colored cards marked "positive," "comparative," "superlative." The first two boxes have separate blue cards for each degree of an adjective. The third box contains orange adverb cards for the words "more," "most," "less," "least," etc., to accompany the blue adjective cards. There should be the correct number of cards for each degree.

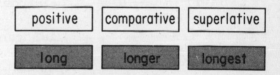

VERB CARDS:

The verb cards are cut from red construction paper in the same way as the noun and adjective cards. There is a neutral-colored card marked "verb" accompanying each group of verb cards.

Make verb cards to go with the farm objects; e.g., runs, sits, jumps, stands, eats.

Make verb cards that your child can act out; e.g., jump, skip, run, wink, sing, dust.

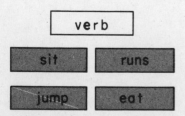

ADVERB CARDS: The adverb cards are cut from orange construction paper in the same way as the cards for the other parts of speech.

Make adverb cards to go with the farm objects; e.g., quietly, cheerfully, quickly, slowly, happily, well.

Make twenty red verb cards and twenty orange adjective cards that can be used together. Examples:

verb	adverb
sing	sweetly
jump	high
dig	deep
eat	quickly

PREPOSITION CARDS: The preposition cards are made from green construction paper. Make a set of preposition cards to go with the farm, using all the prepositions you can think of; e.g., in, to, out, on, up, under, over.

CONJUNCTION CARDS: The conjunction cards are made from purple paper. Make several conjunction cards to go with the farm; e.g., but, and, for.

PRONOUN CARDS:

The pronoun cards are made from pink construction paper. Make pink pronoun cards for the personal pronouns. Using a standard-size sheet of pink construction paper, list the following pronouns.

> I
> you
> he, she, it
> we
> you
> they

PARTS OF SPEECH: THE NOUN PACKET

The noun packets are made up of ten or more 10″ × 4″ cards, cut from white construction paper. Write a sentence at the bottom quarter of each card. Each sentence should contain one or more nouns.

Examples:

> Mars is a planet.
> Hens lay eggs.
> The dog and cat run.

> Hens lay eggs.

> The dog has a ball.

THE ADJECTIVE PACKET

The adjective packets are made as above, but write sentences containing various types of adjectives.

Examples:

> Sarah has some toys.
> This red box is square.
> I like the kind yellow cat.

THE VERB PACKET

The verb packets, made as above, use sentences containing verbs.

Examples:

Katie rode a black horse.
Mother baked a big pie.
Jennifer pulls a wagon.

GRAMMAR SYMBOLS:

Grammar symbols are cut from paper of the same colors as those used for the cards showing parts of speech, e.g., black for nouns, blue for adjectives. Use the geometric patterns illustrated here.

1   2   3

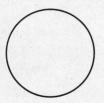

4   5   6

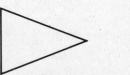 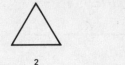

7   8   9

1.	noun	(black)	6.	preposition	(green)
2.	adjective	(royal blue)	7.	pronoun	(purple)
3.	article	(royal blue)	8.	interjection	(yellow)
4.	verb	(red)	9.	conjunction	(pink)
5.	adverb	(orange)			

**GRAMMAR BOXES FOR
PARSING:
BOX 1—NOUN AND
ADJECTIVE**

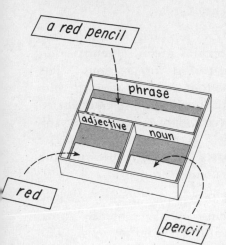

This is a box, approximately 6″ × 4″, which is first divided in half and then the lower half is divided in half again, so that there are three sections. The long section contains blue cards with two phrases on each card, pertaining to objects in the room. One small compartment is labeled with a black card saying "noun," the other compartment with a blue card saying "adjective." The noun compartment contains black cards on which are written all the nouns that will be found on the phrase cards. The adjective section contains blue cards on which are written all the adjectives to be found on the phrase cards.

BOX 2—VERB

This box is made the same way as the noun-and-adjective box. The top half contains red sentence cards, featuring verbs. The bottom half is divided into thirds, with each section labeled accordingly and containing colored cards for the appropriate parts of speech used in the sentence cards.

BOX 3—ADVERB

The top half of this box contains orange sentence cards, featuring adverbs. The bottom half is divided into quarters, with each section labeled accordingly and containing colored cards for the appropriate parts of speech used in the sentence cards.

BOX 4—PREPOSITION

The top half of this box contains green sentence cards, featuring prepositions. The bottom half is divided into fifths, with each section labeled accordingly and containing colored cards for the appropriate parts of speech used in the sentence cards.

BOX 5—CONJUNCTION

The top part of this box contains purple sentence cards, featuring conjunctions. The bottom half has six smaller compartments, labeled accordingly, containing the appropriate colored cards for the parts of speech used in the sentences.

BOX 6—PRONOUN

The top part of this box contains pink sentence cards, featuring pronouns. The bottom half has seven smaller compartments labeled accordingly, containing the appropriate colored cards for the parts of speech used in the sentences.

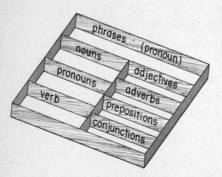

BOX 7—INTERJECTION

The top part of this box contains yellow cards with sentences featuring interjections. The bottom half has eight smaller compartments, labeled accordingly, containing the appropriate colored cards for the parts of speech used in the sentences.

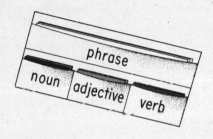

Note: Instead of using boxes, you may use a piece of poster board approximately 9″ × 12″. Make compartments by using construction paper. Divide them just as you would the boxes and label each compartment as illustrated.

EXERCISES

THE ALPHABET SOUNDS

When introducing the alphabet sounds, one often becomes confused over what the exact sound is. In the introduction to sounds, use the sound as it is used in the first sound of the following words:

a *a*pple	g *ga*te	n *n*ot	t *t*op
b *b*at	h *h*at	o *o*ctopus	u *u*mbrella
c *c*at	i *i*n	p *p*in	v *v*ase
d *d*og	j *j*am	q *q*ueen	w *w*eb
e *e*lephant	k *k*ing	r *r*at	x bo*x*
f *f*ish	l *lo*g	s *s*ing	y *y*es
	m *m*ug		z *z*oo

THE MOVABLE ALPHABET
Age 4–6

MATERIAL:

The movable alphabet.
Object boxes with name cards.
Picture cards.

DEMONSTRATION:

1) Let the child familiarize himself with the letters by finding specific alphabet letters as requested.

2) Choose simple three-letter "phonetic" words, say them to the child and have him find the letters he hears in the words.
Example: "What letters do you hear when I say 'dog'?"

3) Continue making words in this way until the child is able to work by himself, using words of his own choice.

4) Give the child a box containing objects with three-letter names.

5) Place each object in turn on the mat, saying its name and building the word with the letters.

6) There should be several such boxes in the room; later he may use boxes containing objects with names having four or more letters.

7) Several boxes of pictures with captions made up of three-letter words should also be available

and used after the object boxes; these will be followed by pictures with more complicated captions.

8) The words may be written after they've been built with the movable alphabet.

PURPOSE: Word analysis as a preparation to reading, writing and spelling. Familiarization with the alphabet.

PHONETICS AND READING
Age 4½–5½

MATERIAL:

Object boxes with name cards.
Picture cards.
Sentence cards.
Picture booklets.

DEMONSTRATION:
STEP I

1) Bring to the table a box of six objects with matching name cards with words having three or four letters.

2) Place the objects on the table.

3) Give the child a name card and ask him to read it aloud (at first he will sound each letter very slowly; ask him to try to say the letters more quickly so that they make a word).

4) Have the child place the card under the corresponding object.

5) Continue in this way until the child understands the exercise and is able to work on his own.

6) The child may then bring other object boxes to the table and work by himself in the same manner.

STEP II

7) Use the same procedure with the picture cards and matching word cards.

8) Introduce the picture cards; have the child match the word cards with the pictures, saying the words aloud.

STEP III

9) Present the descriptive sentence cards; and have the child look at the picture and read the sentence.

STEP IV

10) The child reads the sentences in the small picture booklet by himself. He can later make his own books.

PURPOSE: Introduction to reading.

DIGRAPHS
Age 4½–6½

MATERIAL:

Digraph boxes.
Digraph booklets.
Digraph word lists.
Packets for digraphs.
Two small movable alphabets in contrasting color.

DEMONSTRATION:

1) Introduce the child to each of the digraphs by telling him the sounds.

2) Lay out the material from the digraph box and have the child read the word cards aloud and match them to the correct pictures.

3) Give the child the digraph booklets and have him read the words aloud.

4) Have the child read the lists to notice the different digraphs.

5) Let the child read the words in the digraph packets.

6) The child lays out the pictures and their corresponding name cards. With the two colored alphabets he spells the names out, using one color for the digraph and the other color for the rest of the word.

7) The child may spell the words without benefit of the name cards if he is able, and later he can write them as well.

PURPOSE: Aid to reading and spelling of words following a more complex phonetic rule.

A WORD GAME:
THE SECRET BOX
Age 5–7

MATERIAL: A small box with folded slips of paper containing "phonetic" words of three or more letters.

THE GAME: A child uses this by himself, choosing a slip, opening it and reading the word aloud. He continues in this way with all or as many of the slips as he chooses, asking for help if he needs it. New words can be added from time to time, and don't hesitate to use words that the child might not know.

THE PARTS OF SPEECH
NOUN
Age 4½–6½

MATERIAL
EXERCISE I:

Noun cards with the names of objects in the room.

DEMONSTRATION:

1) This is the child's introduction to grammar and should be introduced parallel with the reading work (e.g., three-letter "phonetic" words, etc.). It is a good group game.

2) Bring to the table the box containing black noun cards, labeled with a neutral-color card marked "noun."

3) Remove the noun card, reading it aloud and casually saying that all the words on the black cards in the box are called nouns.

4) Remove the cards, which should all have names of objects in the room, and read them aloud one at a time.

5) As each card is read, have the child place it with the corresponding object in the room.

6) Begin with a few simple words, then add more.

PURPOSE:

To introduce nouns as names of objects.

MATERIAL
EXERCISE II:

Black noun cards printed with names of family members or people in the room.

DEMONSTRATION:

1) Proceed as above, reading a card, then placing it by the right person.
2) The children can do this themselves, as they usually recognize each other's printed name easily.

PURPOSE:

To introduce nouns as names of people.

MATERIAL
EXERCISE III:

A collection of objects based on a central idea, e.g., a farm. A black noun card with the name of every object in the collection, identified by a neutral-color noun card.

DEMONSTRATION:

1) Your noun cards and objects should be "phonetic." More difficult words may be added later.
2) Place your objects out on the table in any order.

3) Place the neutral-color noun card at the top of the table, then bring out the black cards.

4) One by one, read the cards and have the child place them next to the appropriate object.

PURPOSE:

To strengthen the concept of the noun.

MATERIAL
EXERCISE IV:

Several small baskets or boxes containing folded slips of paper on which is written a familiar noun. Group these according to children's names, flowers, animals. The children may draw these, read them and refold them.

PURPOSE:

To give experiences that lead to a good understanding of the functions of nouns.
To increase vocabulary.

FORMATION OF THE PLURAL
Age 6–9

MATERIAL:

Singular and plural card boxes for all rules.

DEMONSTRATION:

RULE 1

The general rule of adding *s* to the singular.

1) For this exercise only, use the name cards of familiar small objects in the room that can be brought to the table.

2) Open your box of cards and lay out the neutral-color heading cards, "singular," "plural." As you lay out the heading cards, reading them aloud, casually explain that "singular" means one and "plural" means more than one.

3) Lay the first singular card on the table, e.g., stamp. Next to it place a stamp. Now find its plural card, "stamps," and put it opposite the singular card, placing several stamps by it.

4) Continue in this way, using the objects and name cards until the child firmly grasps the idea.

RULE 2

es is added to the singular after a sibilant sound (*s, x, z, sh, ch, ss*).

1) Present the packets of cards for this rule. You needn't explain the rule unless the child asks. He will learn more by seeing than hearing at this stage.

2) Lay the cards out as in the first lesson.

R U L E 3   Words ending in *f, fe* or *lf,* preceded by a long vowel, change to *v* and add *es.*

Present the appropriate singular and plural cards and boxes to illustrate the following rules.

R U L E 4   When *y* is preceded by *qu* or a consonant, change the *y* to *i* and add *es.*

R U L E 5   For most words ending in *o* add *es.*

R U L E 6   The ending *en* is added to the word to make the plural.

R U L E 7   Plurals formed with a vowel change.

R U L E 8   Words remaining the same for the plural.

R U L E 9   Words retaining their foreign form or taking the English spelling. Lay out three columns for these.

P U R P O S E :   To give the child a systematic study of the rules for plurals by letting him see the formations.

THE STUDY OF GENDER
(MASCULINE AND FEMININE)
Age 6–9

MATERIAL: Cards for gender.
Rules for the formation of gender.

RULE 1 The feminine is formed by adding a suffix to the masculine (*ess, ine, trix,* etc.).

RULE 2 The feminine is an entirely different word from the masculine.

RULE 3 A compound word is used to show gender.

DEMONSTRATION:
1) Bring a box for one rule to the table.
2) Lay out the neutral-color heading cards (masculine, feminine).
3) Place the masculine cards under the masculine heading and place their corresponding feminine noun cards under the feminine heading.
4) Read the masculine and feminine nouns aloud.
5) Continue in this way with all the boxes.

PURPOSE: To show the difference in masculine and feminine gender.

THE ADJECTIVE
(ROYAL BLUE)

Age 6–9

**MATERIAL
EXERCISE I:** Materials and objects in the home.

DEMONSTRATION:
1) This can be done with several children together.
2) One by one, ask for certain things to be brought to you. You can say:
"Please bring me the largest pink cube."
"Please bring me the thinnest broad stair."
"Please bring me the roughest board."
"I don't want this green book, please bring me the small yellow one."
"Don't put that cube on the small table, please put it on the large table."

**MATERIAL
EXERCISE II:** The farm objects.
Noun cards to go with farm objects.
Adjective cards to go with farm objects.

DEMONSTRATION:
1) Place the farm animals on the table.
2) Open the noun box and place the noun card on the table. then place

the noun name cards by the appropriate objects.

3) Open the adjective box and place the neutral-color adjective card at the top of the table. Read the adjective cards aloud, one by one, and place them by the appropriate object, e.g., the fat pig, the big horse.

4) Use adjective cards with "phonetic" words at first. Add more adjective cards as the child progresses; for example, you may have more than one adjective card for each of the farm animals (the fat pink pig, the big strong horse).

5) Use the adjective cards for the articles as part of this exercise, explaining that "the" is used to point out the person or object and "a" and "an" are used to indicate amount.

6) More complicated adjectives may be introduced, and new cards may be written as the child suggests them.

MATERIAL EXERCISE III:

A box of twenty noun cards and twenty adjective cards.

DEMONSTRATION:

1) Place the neutral-color noun card at the top of the table.

2) Lay out the noun cards, leaving a space to the left of each one to put the appropriate adjective card.

3) Place the neutral-color adjective card at the top of the table.

4) Place an adjective card in front of each noun card as they are randomly picked out of the box.

5) Have the child read the adjective and noun cards, one by one. As he does so, many will be misplaced and will not make sense.

6) Begin with the first adjective and noun card. If the combination makes sense, leave it; if not, exchange the adjective card for another.

7) Continue in this way until all the noun-and-adjective combinations make sense.

8) Once this is done, take a noun card and place it in front of the child. Ask him to read each adjective card aloud and find all the adjectives that can be used to describe that particular noun (e.g., for "dress"—red, pretty, large, new, etc.) .

9) Do this with several other noun cards, or with all of them if time and interest permit.

MATERIAL
EXERCISE IV: Adjective cards for the three rules of degree of adjectives.

> **Rule 1** Addition of the suffix *er* and *est,* e.g., short, shorter, shortest.
>
> **Rule 2** Irregular formation, e.g., bad, worse, worst.
>
> **Rule 3** Use of the adverbs *more* and *most,* e.g., beautiful, more beautiful, most beautiful.

DEMONSTRATION:
1) The box for Rule 1 is brought to the table.
2) The neutral-color cards, "Positive," "Comparative," "Superlative," are placed at the top of the table.
3) The child arranges the adjective cards below the appropriate cards.
4) Continue in this same way with the boxes for Rule 2 and Rule 3, always reading aloud the words as you place the card on the table.

PURPOSE: To teach the function and importance of the adjective as a descriptive word.

THE VERB
(RED)
Age 6–9

MATERIAL **EXERCISE I:**	The farm objects. Noun, adjective and verb card boxes.
DEMONSTRATION:	1) Set out the farm objects. 2) Place the noun and adjective cards beside the objects. 3) Take the red verb cards, read them one at a time, and place them in the appropriate place, e.g., The fat pink pig *runs*. 4) Continue until all the verb cards are placed, letting the child read aloud the sentence or phrase.
MATERIAL **EXERCISE II:**	Verb cards with words that the child can act out.
DEMONSTRATION:	1) Read the cards and ask one child or a group of children as a whole to do the action. Or the children may take a card, one at a time, read it, and then act it out. 2) After the "phonetic" verb cards have been used and the child knows them, verb cards of more difficult words may be introduced.
PURPOSE:	To teach the function of the verb as an action word. To increase vocabulary.

THE ADVERB
(ORANGE)
Age 6–9

**MATERIAL
EXERCISE I:** A blackboard.

DEMONSTRATION:

1) This is an excellent group game. The group can react as a whole, or a certain child can be given a command.

2) Let the children sit near the blackboard. Tell them that they are to listen quietly while you write things on the board for them to do.

3) Write on the board such sentences as:
Walk to the window slowly.
Walk to the window quietly.

4) Use many sentences asking them to do one specific thing in different ways.

5) Long sentences may be used or short commands, such as:
Clap twice.
Sit quietly.

**MATERIAL
EXERCISE II:** The farm objects.
Boxes of cards for noun, adjective, verb and adverb.

DEMONSTRATION: 1) Proceed in the same way as in the other exercises using the farm objects. But this time add the orange adverb cards.

**MATERIAL
EXERCISE III:** A box of twenty verb cards.
A box of twenty adverb cards.

DEMONSTRATION:
1) Place the verb cards on the table.
2) Place an adverb card in front of each verb card as they are randomly picked from the box.
3) Read the combinations aloud and change the adverb cards if the phrases do not make sense. (This is done in the same way as the noun and adjective exercise.)
4) Then take the verb cards, one at a time, and see how many adverb cards can be used with it, e.g., "walk" slowly, quickly, softly, happily.

PURPOSE: To teach the function and importance of the adverb as a word that tells how something is done.
To increase vocabulary.

THE PREPOSITION
(GREEN)
Age 6–9

MATERIAL
EXERCISE I:

The preposition cards.
The farm objects and corresponding farm cards.

DEMONSTRATION:

1) Place the objects on the table.

2) Make a sentence or phrase with the farm cards, leaving a blank space where the preposition card would go.

3) Place the preposition cards, one by one, in the blank, and by reading them aloud, see if they form a sensible sentence,
   e.g., The goat is *near* the tree.
   The goat is *behind* the tree.

4) As you make the sentences with the cards, move the objects accordingly so the child can immediately grasp the idea of a preposition.

MATERIAL
EXERCISE II:

The farm objects.
The cards for nouns, adjectives, verbs, adverbs and prepositions.

DEMONSTRATION:

1) Place the farm objects on the table.

2) Using the parts of speech learned, form sentences with the word cards, introducing the preposition,

e.g., The pig is standing behind the barn.

3) As sentences are formed, place the objects beside the appropriate words.

PURPOSE: To understand the function and importance of the preposition telling where.

To increase the vocabulary.

THE CONJUNCTION
(PURPLE)
Age 6–9

**MATERIAL
EXERCISE I:**

The conjunction cards.
Several objects in the room.

DEMONSTRATION:

1) Show the child the conjunction card "and" and "but."
2) Talk about two of something,
   e.g., "The dog went outside."
   "The cat went outside."
   "How else could I say that? I could say, the dog AND the cat went outside."
   Or ask the child and let him respond.
3) Repeat this, using other conjunctions,
   e.g., "The dog went outside. The cat stayed inside."
   "The dog went outside, *but* the cat stayed inside."
4) Using objects in the room, illustrate the point further, saying, for example, "The pink cube and the pencil."

**MATERIAL
EXERCISE II:**

The farm objects.
All the word cards.

DEMONSTRATION: 1) Proceeding as in all the previous farm exercises, introduce the conjunction into the sentences formed by the word cards,

e.g., The cow is in the field, *but* the calf is outside.

The man *and* the dog run quickly.

PURPOSE: To demonstrate the function of the conjunction as a joining word.

THE PRONOUN
(PINK)
Age 6–9

MATERIAL
EXERCISE I:

The pronoun cards.
A list of the personal pronouns.

DEMONSTRATION:

1) Explain to the child that if you want to talk about a little girl all the time, you do not have to keep repeating her name. Illustrate this by telling a story without using pronouns.

2) Soon the child will realize that he could be saying "she" instead of always using the proper name (Sarah, for instance).

3) Demonstrate how funny it would sound if you always referred to yourself by name instead of saying "I."

4) Explain that it would be difficult while speaking to a group to have to address each person by name; so, instead, you say, "you."

5) Using the personal pronouns, have the child act out various sentences,

   e.g., *She* sat at the desk.

   You go outside to play.

MATERIAL
EXERCISE II: The pronoun cards.
A list of the personal pronouns.
Verb cards.

DEMONSTRATION: 1) Place the pronoun cards on the table.
2) Place the verbs by the appropriate pronouns.

PURPOSE: To teach the function of the pronoun as a word used to take the place of another.

INTERJECTION
(YELLOW)
Age 6–9

No introduction is necessary to this. Using a sheet of yellow paper, let the child make a list of the common interjections, with your help, and add to it as other words are thought of, e.g., Help! Oh! What! Ouch!

The child will soon realize that it is the tone of voice he uses that makes the word an interjection.

USING SYMBOLS FOR
PARTS OF SPEECH
Age 6–9

MATERIAL	Card packets for the nouns, adjectives and verbs. Envelopes with the symbols for the parts of speech.
DEMONSTRATION:	1) Begin with the noun packet. 2) Place the cards out one at a time, asking the child to point out the nouns. Show him how to put a noun symbol over each. 3) The child may work alone when he understands the procedure. 4) Bring out the adjective packet. 5) Tell him how to place a blue triangle over each adjective, and have him continue to work alone. 6) Bring out the verb packet. 7) The noun symbol is placed over every noun and the adjective symbol over every adjective. 8) Tell the child how to place the verb symbol over every verb and have him continue to work alone. 9) Introduce symbols for the other parts of speech.
PURPOSE:	A study of syntax. The position of each part of speech in the sentence stands out clearly because of its symbol and color.

GRAMMAR BOXES FOR PARSING

Age 6–9

MATERIAL: The seven grammar boxes.
                  Objects named on the noun cards.

DEMONSTRATION:

1) Begin with the first box (nouns and adjectives). *articles*

2) Take out the first card from the long section and read the phrase.

3) Say to the child, as you point to the first word, "What kind of word do you think this is?" (Often they will say, "It's a blue word," rather than "It's an adjective.")

4) If it is an adjective, ask the child to look through the adjective cards in the section of the box and find the word. Take, for example, the phrase card that reads:

   a long pencil
   a short pencil

   When the blue adjective card "a" is found, place it below the phrase card, then find the next word and the next in the appropriate section of the box.

5) Place the three cards below the phrase card, read them aloud, and place the object mentioned next to the cards.

6) Read the second phrase. The first word will be the same, so

leave it. The second word needs changing. Remove it and place it upside down on the table so that the child will not use it again.

7) Find the new adjective card and place it in the empty space. Leave the word "pencil" as it is.

8) Now read the new phrase aloud, and place the proper object next to the cards.

9) Remind the child of what the parts of speech are. (Pointing to the blue card: "What do we call this word?" Child: "Adjective," and so on.)

10) After the initial introduction, the child can work alone.

11) After the child has built the sentences with the individual cards, change the position of the cards and let him read the result, then try to change the position of the words to make sense. (This is a good lesson in syntax.)

12) Each of the other grammar boxes are introduced in the same way. The child works alone after the introduction.

13) Depending on the enthusiasm of the child, the phrase or sentence cards may be changed and new ones added.

PURPOSE:

To teach the names of the parts of speech and clarify their function. Introduction to parsing.

COMMANDS
(WITH GRAMMAR SYMBOLS)
Age 6–9

MATERIAL:

Grammar symbols.
Slips of paper to write phrases, words, sentences.

DEMONSTRATION:

1) On a piece of paper, write a simple command,
   e.g., "Stand and sing."

2) The child reads and performs the command.

3) Ask the child how many actions he performed. When he answers, "Two," ask him to put red circles on top of the words that told him what to do.

4) Now tear the piece of paper and reverse the command, "Sing and stand."

5) Again the child sees the action words. Then reconstruct the sentence.

6) The child can work alone with slips of paper with commands already written on them. He reads the command, and finds how many actions are involved. A red circle is placed on each verb.

7) As the child understands the process, use more complicated sentences,
e.g., "Walk to the window and close it."

8) Later the child can write the commands for himself.

PURPOSE: Indirect preparation for sentence syntax and analysis.

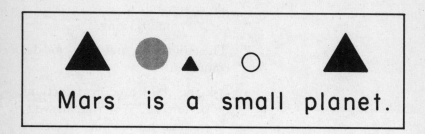

□

Appendix

MATHEMATICS

0	1	2	3	4	5	6	7	8	9
1	2	3	4	5	6	7	8	9	10
2	3	4	5	6	7	8	9	10	11
3	4	5	6	7	8	9	10	11	12
4	5	6	7	8	9	10	11	12	13
5	6	7	8	9	10	11	12	13	14
6	7	8	9	10	11	12	13	14	15
7	8	9	10	11	12	13	14	15	16
8	9	10	11	12	13	14	15	16	17
9	10	11	12	13	14	15	16	17	18

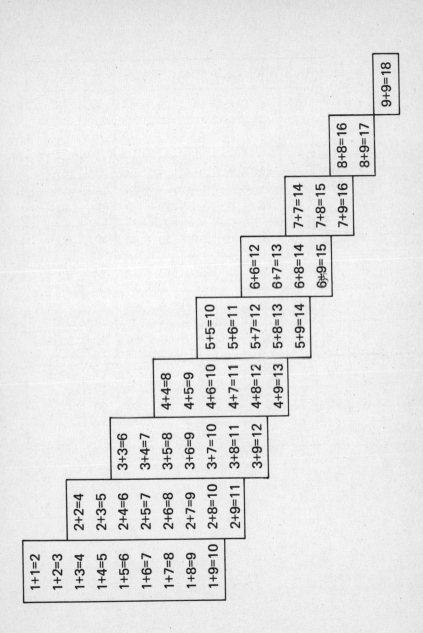

TABLE OF PYTHAGORAS

1	2	3	4	5	6	7	8	9	10
2	4	6	8	10	12	14	16	18	20
3	6	9	12	15	18	21	24	27	30
4	8	12	16	20	24	28	32	36	40
5	10	15	20	25	30	35	40	45	50
6	12	18	24	30	36	42	48	54	60
7	14	21	28	35	42	49	56	63	70
8	16	24	32	40	48	56	64	72	80
9	18	27	36	45	54	63	72	81	90
10	20	30	40	50	60	70	80	90	100

1 x 1 = 1	2 x 1 = 2	3 x 1 = 3
1 x 2 = 2	2 x 2 = 4	3 x 2 = 6
1 x 3 = 3	2 x 3 = 6	3 x 3 = 9
1 x 4 = 4	2 x 4 = 8	3 x 4 = 12
1 x 5 = 5	2 x 5 = 10	3 x 5 = 15
1 x 6 = 6	2 x 6 = 12	3 x 6 = 18
1 x 7 = 7	2 x 7 = 14	3 x 7 = 21
1 x 8 = 8	2 x 8 = 16	3 x 8 = 24
1 x 9 = 9	2 x 9 = 18	3 x 9 = 27

4 x 1 = 4	5 x 1 = 5	6 x 1 = 6
4 x 2 = 8	5 x 2 = 10	6 x 2 = 12
4 x 3 = 12	5 x 3 = 15	6 x 3 = 18
4 x 4 = 16	5 x 4 = 20	6 x 4 = 24
4 x 5 = 20	5 x 5 = 25	6 x 5 = 30
4 x 6 = 24	5 x 6 = 30	6 x 6 = 36
4 x 7 = 28	5 x 7 = 35	6 x 7 = 42
4 x 8 = 32	5 x 8 = 40	6 x 8 = 48
4 x 9 = 36	5 x 9 = 45	6 x 9 = 54

7 x 1 = 7	8 x 1 = 8	9 x 1 = 9
7 x 2 = 14	8 x 2 = 16	9 x 2 = 18
7 x 3 = 21	8 x 3 = 24	9 x 3 = 27
7 x 4 = 28	8 x 4 = 32	9 x 4 = 36
7 x 5 = 35	8 x 5 = 40	9 x 5 = 45
7 x 6 = 42	8 x 6 = 48	9 x 6 = 54
7 x 7 = 49	8 x 7 = 56	9 x 7 = 63
7 x 8 = 56	8 x 8 = 64	9 x 8 = 72
7 x 9 = 63	8 x 9 = 72	9 x 9 = 81

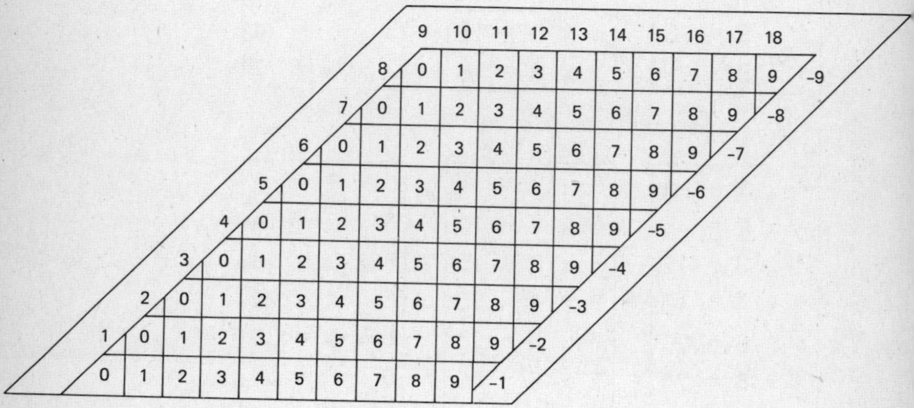
9 10 11 12 13 14 15 16 17 18
8 0 1 2 3 4 5 6 7 8 9 -9
7 0 1 2 3 4 5 6 7 8 9 -8
6 0 1 2 3 4 5 6 7 8 9 -7
5 0 1 2 3 4 5 6 7 8 9 -6
4 0 1 2 3 4 5 6 7 8 9 -5
3 0 1 2 3 4 5 6 7 8 9 -4
2 0 1 2 3 4 5 6 7 8 9 -3
1 0 1 2 3 4 5 6 7 8 9 -2
0 1 2 3 4 5 6 7 8 9 -1

1-1=0																
	2-2=0															
	2-1=1															
		3-3=0														
		3-2=1														
		3-1=2														
			4-4=0													
			4-3=1													
			4-2=2													
			4-1=3													
				5-5=0												
				5-4=1												
				5-3=2												
				5-2=3												
				5-1=4												
					6-6=0											
					6-5=1											
					6-4=2											
					6-3=3											
					6-2=4											
					6-1=5											
						7-7=0										
						7-6=1										
						7-5=2										
						7-4=3										
						7-3=4										
						7-2=5										
						7-1=6										
							8-8=0									
							8-7=1									
							8-6=2									
							8-5=3									
							8-4=4									
							8-3=5									
							8-2=6									
							8-1=7									
								9-9=0	10-9=1	11-9=2	12-9=3	13-9=4	14-9=5	15-9=6	16-9=7	17-9=8
								9-8=1	10-8=2	11-8=3	12-8=4	13-8=5	14-8=6	15-8=7	16-8=8	17-8=9
								9-7=2	10-7=3	11-7=4	12-7=5	13-7=6	14-7=7	15-7=8	16-7=9	
								9-6=3	10-6=4	11-6=5	12-6=6	13-6=7	14-6=8	15-6=9		
								9-5=4	10-5=5	11-6=6	12-5=7	13-5=8	14-5=9			
								9-4=5	10-4=6	11-4=7	12-4=8	13-4=9				
								9-3=6	10-3=7	11-3=8	12-3=9					
								9-2=7	10-2=8	11-2=9						
								9-1=8	10-1=9							

	÷9	÷8	÷7	÷6	÷5	÷4	÷3	÷2	÷1
1									1
2								1	2
3							1		3
4						1		2	4
5					1				5
6				1			2	3	6
7			1						7
8		1				2		4	8
9	1						3		9
10					2			5	
12				2		3	4	6	
14			2					7	
15					3		5		
16		2				4		8	
18	2			3			6	9	
20					4	5			
21			3				7		
24		3		4		6	8		
25					5				
27	3						9		
28			4			7			
30				5	6				
32		4				8			
35			5		7				
36	4			6		9			
40		5			8				
42			6	7					
45	5				9				
48		6		8					
49			7						
54	6			9					
56		7	8						
63	7		9						
64		8							
72	8	9							
81	9								

2 ÷ 2 = 1	3 ÷ 3 = 1
4 ÷ 2 = 2	6 ÷ 3 = 2
6 ÷ 2 = 3	9 ÷ 3 = 3
8 ÷ 2 = 4	12 ÷ 3 = 4
10 ÷ 2 = 5	15 ÷ 3 = 5
12 ÷ 2 = 6	18 ÷ 3 = 6
14 ÷ 2 = 7	21 ÷ 3 = 7
16 ÷ 2 = 8	24 ÷ 3 = 8
18 ÷ 2 = 9	27 ÷ 3 = 9

```
2 ÷ 2 = 1        3 ÷ 3 = 1        4 ÷ 4 = 1        5 ÷ 5 = 1
4 ÷ 2 = 2        6 ÷ 3 = 2        8 ÷ 4 = 2       10 ÷ 5 = 2
6 ÷ 2 = 3        9 ÷ 3 = 3       12 ÷ 4 = 3       15 ÷ 5 = 3
8 ÷ 2 = 4       12 ÷ 3 = 4       16 ÷ 4 = 4       20 ÷ 5 = 4
10 ÷ 2 = 5      15 ÷ 3 = 5       20 ÷ 4 = 5       25 ÷ 5 = 5
12 ÷ 2 = 6      18 ÷ 3 = 6       24 ÷ 4 = 6       30 ÷ 5 = 6
14 ÷ 2 = 7      21 ÷ 3 = 7       28 ÷ 4 = 7       35 ÷ 5 = 7
16 ÷ 2 = 8      24 ÷ 3 = 8       32 ÷ 4 = 8       40 ÷ 5 = 8
18 ÷ 2 = 9      27 ÷ 3 = 9       36 ÷ 4 = 9       45 ÷ 5 = 9


 6 ÷ 6 = 1        7 ÷ 7 = 1        8 ÷ 8 = 1        9 ÷ 9 = 1
12 ÷ 6 = 2       14 ÷ 7 = 2       16 ÷ 8 = 2       18 : 9 = 2
18 ÷ 6 = 3       21 ÷ 7 = 3       24 ÷ 8 = 3       27 ÷ 9 = 3
24 ÷ 6 = 4       28 ÷ 7 = 4       32 ÷ 8 = 4       36 ÷ 9 = 4
30 ÷ 6 = 5       35 ÷ 7 = 5       40 ÷ 8 = 5       45 ÷ 9 = 5
36 ÷ 6 = 6       42 ÷ 7 = 6       48 ÷ 8 = 6       54 ÷ 9 = 6
42 ÷ 6 = 7       49 ÷ 7 = 7       56 ÷ 8 = 7       63 ÷ 9 = 7
48 ÷ 6 = 8       56 ÷ 7 = 8       64 ÷ 8 = 8       72 ÷ 9 = 8
54 ÷ 6 = 9       63 ÷ 7 = 9       72 ÷ 8 = 9       81 ÷ 9 = 9
```

□

Appendix
LANGUAGE

WORD LISTS

FOR USE WITH EXERCISES

"PHONETIC" WORDS

a			**e**		
act	gap	rap	bed	kept	spend
am	gas	sad	beg	leg	steps
an	glad	sat	belt	let	test
ant	grand	sand	bend	lent	tent
as	had	sank	best	melt	west
bad	ham	snap	bet	men	vet
bag	hand	stag	crept	met	web
band	has	stamp	den	peg	wet
bang	hat	stand	dent	pen	went
bank	jam	tax	desk	pest	wept
bat	lad	trap	egg	pet	west
brag	lap	van	elf	red	
camp	lamp	wag	end	rent	
can	land		elm	rest	
cat	mad		fed	set	
clap	man		felt	self	
crab	pan		fled	send	
fan	pat		get	sent	
fat	plank		hem	stem	
flag	rag		jet	slept	
gag	ran		keg	swept	

i

bib	ink	silk
big	is	sing
bin	jig	skin
bit	kid	sink
brim	king	swim
dig	lid	twig
dim	lift	twist
dip	link	twin
drink	lit	win
film	mix	
fin	milk	
fit	pig	
first	pin	
fix	pink	
gift	red	
hid	rip	
him	ring	
hint	six	
hit	sit	
if	sip	

o

box	nod
cot	ox
crop	of
clock	pot
dog	pop
doll	plot
dot	rod
drop	romp
fog	sock
fox	sod
frog	soft
frost	spot
from	
hog	
hop	
job	
jog	
lost	
mop	
not	

u

bud	jug
bun	just
bus	jump
but	lump
bulb	mug
cub	mud
cup	must
crust	nut
club	pup
clump	plum
dug	pump
drum	rub
fun	rut
gun	rust
gum	sum
glum	sung
grunt	tub
gust	tug
hut	trumpet
hum	trust
hunt	us
hump	

SINGULARS AND PLURALS

	Singular	*Plural*
RULE 1	lid	lids
	dog	dogs
	tray	trays
RULE 2	church	churches
	box	boxes
	bench	benches
	class	classes
	watch	watches
RULE 3	half	halves
	leaf	leaves
	elf	elves
	knife	knives
RULE 4	penny	pennies
	fly	flies
RULE 5	potato	potatoes
	zero	zeroes
RULE 6	child	children
	ox	oxen
	brother	brethren
RULE 7	man	men
	mouse	mice
	foot	feet
	goose	geese
RULE 8	fish	fish
	deer	deer

	Singular	*Plural*	*Plural*
RULE 9	hippopotamus	hippopotamuses	hippopotami
	cactus	cactuses	cacti
	cherub	cherubs	cherubim

GENDER

	Masculine	Feminine
RULE 1	lion	lioness
	prince	princess
	waiter	waitress
	aviator	aviatrix
	executor	executrix
	usher	usherette
	hero	heroine
RULE 2	father	mother
	uncle	aunt
	cock	hen
	ram	ewe
	king	queen
RULE 3	landlord	landlady
	son-in-law	daughter-in-law
	grandfather	grandmother
	he-bear	she-bear
	peacock	peahen

DEGREES OF ADJECTIVES

Positive	Comparative	Superlative
long	longer	longest
old	older	oldest
fat	fatter	fattest
good	better	best
many	more	most
little	less	least
bad	worse	worst
wonderful	more wonderful	most wonderful
beautiful	more beautiful	most beautiful

DIGRAPHS AND
FAMILIAR COMBINATIONS

ai	ay	a-e
rain	day	flake
pail	say	gate
train	play	cake
paint	sway	brave
waist	crayon	made
snail	tray	ate
pain	pray	state

ea	ee	ie
meat	bee	field
leaf	feed	priest
dream	tree	pier
eat	feet	tier
squeak	green	
beast	sleep	
bead	coffee	
seat	weep	

oa	ow	o-e
soap	grow	rope
boat	pillow	smoke
coat	snow	come
toad	blow	home
loaf	sorrow	robe
foam	low	joke
toast	follow	pole
oats	glow	

ue	ew	u-e
blue	few	cube
glue	drew	tube
issue	blew	costume
rescue	jewel	rule
true	new	fume
duel	grew	

ow

how
drown
cow
clown

ou

mouse
house
round
count
spout

oy

boy
toy
employ
destroy
joy

oi

poison
point
soil
avoid
oil

ir

bird
skirt
girl
dirt

er

fern
butter
letter
person
ladder

ur

fur
burst
turf
disturb
burn

oo

moon
spoon
balloon
loop
stool

oo

cook
brook
wool
good
foot

au

haul
clause
fault

aw

raw
lawn
shawl
straw
saw

ck

sack
truck
kick
sock
pack
luck

ch

ache
anchor
echo
chorus

ch

chop
chair
much
lunch
bench
patch
witch

sh

shovel
ship
shed
ash
cash
fish
dish
shell

th

think
thing
depth
tenth
them
moth

wh

when
whistle
white
whip
whirl

ph

telephone
elephant
prophet
sphinx

qu

quill
queen
liquid
request
quilt
equip

SUGGESTED READING

A SELECTION OF BOOKS ABOUT THE MONTESSORI METHOD OF EDUCATION

Dr. Montessori wrote numerous books covering her work with children, her philosophy and her teaching method. Now in the public domain, her books have been printed and reprinted repeatedly in the past ten years. Many of them are in paperback editions. Some of Dr. Montessori's writings are complex, others are somewhat repetitious of her previous works. For this reason I have listed only a small selection, which I feel covers all of the areas on which she wrote, with a minimum of overlapping ideas. I have also included some helpful and informative books written by others concerned with the Montessori approach to learning.

Fisher, Dorothy Canfield, *Montessori for Parents*, rev. ed. Cambridge, Massachusetts, Robert Bentley, Inc., 1965.
Originally titled *Montessori Mother*, this book was written after the author's visit to the Casa dei Bambini in the early 1900's. The method, materials and a layman's interpretations give much insight to Dr. Montessori's ideas.

Hainstock, Elizabeth G., *Teaching Montessori in the Home*. New York, Random House, 1968.
A practical approach to introducing the Montessori method into the home environment. A handbook for mothers, with complete instructions for making and using the materials easily and enjoyably.

Montessori, Maria, *The Secret of Childhood*, rev. ed. Notre Dame, Indiana, Fides Publishers, Inc., 1966.
Maria Montessori discusses her philosophy and states the value of the child's contribution to humanity, if we will but take time to understand and respect him.

Montessori, Maria, *The Absorbent Mind*, rev. ed. New York, Dell Publishing Co., 1967.
A description of the years from birth to age six, and the physical and psychological aspects of growth and development.

Montessori, Maria, *Dr. Montessori's Own Handbook*. New York, Schocken Books, 1965.
A definition of the Montessori method, with descriptions of the materials and their purpose, as well as the role of the child and the teacher.

Montessori, Maria, *The Montessori Method*. Cambridge, Massachusetts, Robert Bentley, Inc., 1965.
An introduction to Dr. Montessori's theories in education and her early work with the children in the first Casa dei Bambini.

Orem, R. C., *Montessori for the Disadvantaged*. New York, G. P. Putnam's Sons, 1967.
A collection of ideas by contributing educators for the application of Montessori principles to poverty programs.

Rambusch, Nancy McCormick, *Learning How to Learn*. Baltimore, Maryland, Helicon Press, 1962.
"An American approach to Montessori" by the founder of Whitby School, stressing the lack of understanding of the nature of children and what we can do about it.

St. Nicholas' Training Centre for the Montessori Method of Education, Correspondence Course, 23 Princes Gate, London, England.

Standing, E. M., *Maria Montessori: Her Life and Work*, Fresno, California, Academy Guild Press, 1959.
A complete and detailed biography of Dr. Montessori written by a devoted disciple and friend.